MUAY THAI FIGHTER

PUBLISHED IN 2012 BY MAVERICK HOUSE PUBLISHERS.
Maverick House, Office 19, Dunboyne Business Park, Dunboyne,
Co. Meath, Ireland.
Maverick House Asia, Level 43, United Centre, 323 Silom Road, Bangrak,
Bangkok 10500, Thailand.

info@maverickhouse.com
http://www.maverickhouse.com

ISBN: 978-1-908518-33-0

5 4 3 2 1

The paper used in this book comes from wood pulp of managed forests.
For every tree felled, at least one tree is planted, thereby renewing natural
resources.

The moral rights of the authors have been asserted.

A CIP catalogue record for this book is available from the British Library.

MUAY THAI FIGHTER

A Farang's Journey to Become a Thai Boxer

Paul Garrigan

Chapter 1

THE ASSAULT DID NOT EASE up. My attacker surely knew all the fight had been knocked out of me but he kept on coming. I would have put my hands up in surrender if I thought it would make any difference. The sneer on his face left no room for pity; he wanted to cause me even more pain. I could see that. He barely knew me yet he showed all the signs of wanting to kill me. I'd obviously given him a particularly bad first impression.

I staggered as his hook made contact with the left side of my temple; another punch I'd not seen coming. I tried to raise my hands higher to protect my head, but my arms were getting tired. I wondered if now would be a good time to just collapse. Somewhere from the back of my mind came the knowledge that my lack of energy must be a result of an adrenalin dump; the stress of the fight or flight response had just eaten up all my reserves.

I stayed with my head slightly bowed and both my fists against my forehead. I looked out from between my arms. I could no longer bring myself to look into the eyes of my attacker because the intensity there intimidated me so much. Instead I just kept staring at his chest and tried to imagine being up against a puzzle rather than a person trying to hurt me. Maybe if I could just regain some composure, and figure out a strategy, I would be able to escape this fight without being seriously injured. I sent out a jab in the hope that it would drive him back, but he easily absorbed my ineffective strike. He responded with a flurry of hooks that almost knocked me unconscious. I now felt physically sick.

I flung my arms around his neck in the hope that this would put an end to the punches to my head. If I soaked up many more of them it might lead to some type of permanent brain damage. Holding on to him seemed to require less energy than keeping my guard up, so for a couple of seconds it felt like I had been given a reprieve. Normally I would feel a bit uncomfortable being so close to another man. I could feel his breath on my skin and his sweat mixed with my own. Such discomfort meant nothing to me now. I tried to hold him tighter than I'd ever attempted with any girlfriend.

His knee hit my side hard but I didn't ease up on my grip. My forehead rested on his shoulder, and I tried to move my hips closer to his. Maybe if I could get my body completely against his he would not be able to knee me so easily. He somehow managed to step back and create a gap between us large enough to allow him to send a knee right into my stomach; he knocked the wind out of me. The shock of this caused me to loosen my grip around his neck. I made the mistake of looking directly in his face; if looks could kill. I offered him a trembling smile in the hope that this would remind him of my humanity. It had no impact as once again he returned to pounding my head.

Out of desperation I flung a couple of my own wild hooks in his direction. I tried to summon up some anger in the hope that this would give me some strength. I couldn't find such power and my attack had a pathetic quality to it that would not pose any threat to my opponent. I tried a right turning kick to his head; surprising myself by finding the energy to do this. He reacted by sweeping my left leg from under me; my arse hit the mat with a thud. The effortless way that he had managed to do this only emphasised my ineptness.

My opponent hovered above me, bouncing on his toes. He looked down impatiently as if I had selected to take this impromptu break from the battering. I didn't want to get up because he couldn't touch me while I lay on the ground; this wasn't mixed martial arts after all. I looked over at the clock and saw 1:07 left. If this had been a competition fight the referee would already have begun counting me out. I wouldn't have minded that. Instead a trainer came over and pulled me to my feet so that my opponent could continue to use me as a punch bag.

I tried to comfort myself with the idea that surviving one more minute wasn't such a big deal. I would just stay tucked behind my guard and weather the storm. I wouldn't even waste my time trying to attack. I again bowed forward but this time my fists reached right to the back of my head; I would sacrifice my stomach to protect my face and brain. My opponent must have also realised that time was almost up; he attacked me with added ferocity. Punches came from every direction; one of them made contact with my ear and that produced a new kind of buzzing pain. I wondered if a gloved hand could cause a burst ear drum.

I looked appealingly at the trainer. Surely he must see how I am getting demolished here. I appreciated that Muay Thai involved a lot of physical contact, but I'd been led to believe that people were meant to take it easy while sparring; especially when they were up against a novice like me. My opponent seemed to be under the impression that his life depended on not holding anything back. The trainer didn't appear to be the least bit bothered by the onslaught; maybe I'd done something to piss him off as well. As the clock ticked down to zero the awareness of the stupidity of putting myself in such a position also hit me hard.

Chapter 2

ALL DRUNKS HAVE A HARD luck story. It helps them make sense of their fall into despair. To other people it may sound like a weak attempt to justify the inexcusable; sometimes it will even sound that way to the narrator, at least it did for me. All humans use narratives to explain their current situation. Addicts cling to such stories as if they were life rafts.

My hard luck story involved martial arts. As a teenager I replaced this training with drinking; a decision I'd lament when I became drunkenly sentimental. My fellow boozers never paid my tale of woe much gravitas, but I meant every word of it. It had been the path away from martial arts that led me straight into addiction. I'm convinced of that. It does not surprise me to find that my journey away from drunkenness has led me right back to martial arts.

I had been a drunk for almost two decades, but I did have sober periods. I hit my first rehab clinic at twenty years old and stayed booze free for eight months. During that time I returned to a daily practice of martial arts, but I never returned to class. In my mid twenties I managed to get off the grog for two whole years. I took up Tai Chi and fell in love with the graceful movements of this gentle Chinese combat system. There were also many brief periods of sobriety that lasted anything from a couple of weeks to a few months. During each of these dry patches I'd try to get back into at least some type of solo martial arts training.

When I finally gave up alcohol I'd reached my mid thirties and lived in Thailand. I see it as a real stroke of luck that I got sober in one of the best places in the world to learn martial arts. I never planned it that way. I would love to tell people that it was Muay Thai that attracted me to Thailand, but it wasn't like that at all. I'd been working in Saudi Arabia and only came to South East Asia on holiday. My reason for going to live in the desert was the illegality of alcohol in that part of the world. I thought it would help me give up my addiction. It didn't, and I disliked working there. I had no good reason to return to Saudi so I stayed on in South East Asia. I ended up on one of the Thai islands and from there fell into teaching English to school kids in Bangkok. Ten years later and I'm still here.

Thoughts of learning Muay Thai niggled at me for a long time. When I was drinking it was easy to dismiss such ideas as foolishness. The urge to give it a go followed me into sobriety; the notion both excited and frightened me. I'd already decided that martial arts would be something that I'd take up again in recovery, but Muay Thai seemed a bit out of my league. I'd been thinking of rekindling my interest in Tai Chi or possibly taking up a soft style of Kung Fu. Even as a teenager I would have balked at the idea of learning such a tough form of combat like Muay Thai – so what business did I have even considering it in middle age? During my first few years sober I returned to a not so regular solo practice that included the few techniques from Kung Fu I could still remember mixed with a bit of Tai Chi.

The death of my father gave me the push I needed to give Muay Thai a go. I wasn't able to go to his funeral back in Ireland; I'd already said my goodbyes. A return to martial arts felt like a more appropriate way to remember him. This had been an activity we enjoyed doing together. I loved my dad, but it was during those years practising martial arts together that we had been closest. For years I'd sort of partially blamed him for my move from Kung Fu to alcoholism, but that had just been part of my hard luck story. I'd chosen my own path, and I earned the fruits of this.

I didn't really know that much about Muay Thai. I'd had a brief encounter with this martial art in my teens, and sometimes I'd watch it on Thai TV. I'd only made it to a couple of live fights; on both of these occasions I'd been too drunk to fully appreciate the skill involved. I did know that behind the modern sport lay a martial art that had once been used in war to defend Thailand. I'd no idea about what the actual training might involve.

I had no real interest in getting involved in the sports element of Muay Thai. At that time I didn't even know it would be possible for someone my age to enter competitions. I felt attracted to the more traditional aspects of the training. I'd seen a few Thai movies where this had been on display, and it impressed the hell out of me. That is what I wanted to learn.

My goal in learning a martial art is not self-defence. I am attracted to the physical training, and the benefits this brings to my body, but it is the mental development side of things that most interests me. In Japanese

Buddhism they call this Mushin which translates as 'empty mind'. Athletes in western countries refer to the same experience as 'flow'. Those who achieve such a state feel like they have become one with the movements they are performing so that it is like they have entered a meditative state. Those who have developed Mushin learn how to live in the moment without the need to change anything; they are better able to embrace the mystery of life. I wanted some of that Mushin for myself.

So I was looking for a martial art that would help me increase my physical fitness as well as cultivating my mind. Meditation had become a hugely important part of my life already, but I could see that it needed to be combined with some type of physical practice. This is how Shaolin Kung Fu came about. Apparently the original exercises were invented so that the Buddhist monks could stay fit as this would enable them to meditate more effectively. Just sitting cross-legged all day can make people sick so some type of physical practice benefits any spiritual path.

I suppose it would have been logical for me to return to Tai Chi as this offers a good mix of health benefits along with mental development practice. It didn't really feel suitable now because I wanted something that would be more of a challenge; there is a lot less cardiovascular training in Tai Chi than other martial arts. I'd hit middle age so this would be my last chance to develop a high level of physical fitness. I wanted to see how far I could progress in this regard. Muay Thai seemed to fit the bill perfectly.

Chapter 3

EVEN AFTER I'D MADE THE decision to give Muay Thai a go I still delayed. My fitness level was the excuse. I'd let myself go a bit since moving into a career as a freelance writer. I spent most of the day sitting down at the computer. My diet also left a lot to be desired. I'd turn to food in much the same way as I once did to alcohol. Since giving up the booze my weight had been up and down. At the time it was very much on the up – over 82kg. I continued to do a bit of solo martial arts practice, but these sessions rarely lasted more than ten minutes.

Turning into a slob crept up on me. I'd been skinny right up until my thirties. I once used to drink high calorie supplements in the hope of putting on a few kilograms. As I got older there was no longer any need for this. The scary thing was that I put on so much weight without even noticing. I've never been really obese but carrying extra weight just looks a bit ridiculous with my small frame. It also depressed me because I did not give up a life of alcohol abuse just to become an unhealthy fatty.

My initial plan involved getting back in shape before going to my first Muay Thai class. Beginning training without building up to it first sounded painful. I had no experience of what went on in a Muay Thai class in Thailand, but I felt certain that it was going to involve a lot of physical effort. If I got back in shape first this would make my transition into the training a bit easier.

I went on YouTube to see if I could find out more information about what happened at a typical Muay Thai class. I found thousands of videos on the subject. Many gave brief glimpses of the training in Thailand experience. These were movies made by people who had come here to train. All the stars of these videos looked to be in top physical shape. I couldn't find one of a middle aged plump guy who was struggling with his fitness. I later found out that there were a few videos like this, but during that particular hunt through YouTube it was only the peak fitness guys that caught my attention. It worried me.

I'd bought a punch bag a few weeks before and had this hung up outside in our kitchen area. I say kitchen but it is just a tiny yard with a roof overhead to keep the rain off. It is common in Thailand to have the cooking area outside. It's a good idea because it means that food smells don't stink up the house. There was enough room in the yard for me to use some of the area as a gym. The overhead rafter turned out to be ideal for hanging the bag. My wife worried that the extra weight might bring this roof down, but it looked sturdy enough – not that I'm any expert when it comes to construction.

My fitness routine involved hitting this bag with kicks and punches for as long as I could. On my first attempt I lasted about seven minutes. I had to stop. Not only was I unable to breathe, but my knuckles were bleeding. Not surprising really as I hadn't yet invested in a pair of gloves. I'd settled for the idea of gently conditioning my knuckles on the canvas. I hadn't expected that doing this would mean that my fist would develop what looked like leprosy sores after just a few minutes of punching the bag.

I'd also bought a skipping rope because I'd heard they did a lot of this type of stamina exercise in the Muay Thai training camps. I hadn't used a rope in decades but assumed it was like riding a bicycle. It turned out to be a lot harder than expected. My feet would get caught in the rope every few turns. After about two minutes it felt like I'd run a marathon. I'd heard that they would skip for as much as 30 minutes in the gym so my lack of stamina for this activity worried me greatly.

I continued with the bag and skipping rope for a couple of weeks, but it didn't feel like the ideal solution to building up my fitness. I needed something more. I had tried to take up running a few times since getting sober, but always gave up after a few outings. I'd pick up a minor injury or just give up out of laziness. I blamed the Thai heat and bad roads; running just felt too much like hard work. I'd be enthusiastic for the first few days but then my motivation would wane. I had once really loved running, but it just didn't fit the Thai conditions – or at least this is what I told myself. I'd seen other people running so this meant my excuses sometimes appeared a bit lame even to me.

I've not had much experience with cycling as an adult, but it certainly looked like a nice way to get fit. One thing that would bug me about running in Thailand was the number of people who would stop to offer me a lift in their vehicle. This happened most when I lived in rural Phitsanulok. One benefit of cycling is that it looks a bit more purposeful. The locals would be less likely to stop me to check if I was lost or having some type of mental breakdown.

I mentioned the bike idea to my wife, but she wasn't impressed. We'd been together eight years and Oa had seen it all before. I've bought enough exercise equipment over the years to fill a reasonably sized gym. My enthusiasm for these new purchases doesn't usually last long. It seems that there is no fitness gadget out there that does away with the need for motivation and persistence.

My only successful fitness expenditure had been the Nintendo Wii with fitness pack. This had been a huge investment for me at the time. My wife had been sceptical about that purchase too, but I used it religiously for almost a year. During that time I brought my weight down from 86kg to 73kg. A lot of the credit for the weight loss could be attributed to my diet, but this game console certainly played a part. I enjoyed exercising in front of the TV, and for a long time it seemed as if my fitness problems were behind me. One day the batteries went dead in the balance board, but instead of replacing them, like I normally did, I just stopped using it. A year later, and I'm out of shape and back up to 82kg.

Despite Oa's misgivings about the bike she allowed my enthusiasm to win her over. It normally works that way. I get the urge to buy something, and pester Oa until she agrees that it is a good idea. She hardly ever spends money on herself, but she worries when I spend too much. This is understandable because we have a child now, and I've a bad history of being reckless with money. She would never stop me buying something, but I like her to approve. This never bothered me before our son arrived on the scene.

I bought a bike in one of the local department stores. It was cheap at only 2,000 THB (about 50 Euros). I knew at that price it wasn't going to get me into the Tour de France, but it would probably be adequate for my purposes. In the excitement of buying my new toy I never considered how I'd fit it into my car. In the end I hired a songthaew (a pick-up truck that is used as a bus) to take it back for me.

Chapter 4

IT WASN'T COMPLETELY MY FAULT that the bike idea didn't work out. The local dog population deserves a lot of the credit. The first couple of trips on the bike were wonderful. The seat felt a bit hard on my arse but nothing unbearable. My first outing lasted for over an hour. We'd only recently moved to Minburi. I'd only had the opportunity to use the main local roads, but this new form of transportation gave me a chance to really explore my new neighbourhood. I would set out in the early morning, and this meant the sun hadn't yet warmed things up too much. The local traffic would also be light enough that it didn't bother me on these trips.

When I got home after that first bike ride my enthusiasm for cycling knew no bounds. I became an instant convert. I even put together a flattering post about it for my blog. I regretted waiting so long to discover the joys of bikes, but I would make up for it now. Here was the answer to my agnostic prayers; an effortless way to get physically in shape. I predicted that a month of cycling combined with the punch bag would get me ready for my first Muay Thai class.

I'd heard other people complain about them, but up until this point I'd never had a problem with Thai dogs.

If someone got bitten I'd assume it was their own fault. They had obviously shown fear. I liked dogs, and liked to think that they liked me too. On the rare occasions when a dog growled at me I'd just growl back – this strategy always worked well enough for me.

One of the first things our new neighbours told us was to watch out for the dogs. It turns out that almost all the locals had been bitten at one time or another. Apparently an elderly woman who lived on the opposite road had only recently been attacked. She was in her seventies but could still ride a bike daily. I greatly admire this type of spirit. This inspirational woman had been riding along when one of the local mutts leaped at her. She fell off the bike, and now felt afraid to leave the house. I found the story upsetting; it seemed so unfair that this woman should have her independence taken away from her like that. Once again I put it down to her showing fear to the dogs. It did annoy me though. I thought we were moving somewhere that my son would be safe to walk around.

We have a beautiful artificial lake in our housing estate. It is covered in lotus leaves, and it is possible to catch glimpses of fish just below the surface. One of the first things I did when we moved in was take my son for a walk to check out the lake. We had only made it to the end of our road when we were faced by a pack of barking dogs. I wasn't intimidated by them but I knew my son would get upset if they continued to be aggressive so I reluctantly turned back.

It was my third trip out on the bike when I had my first run in with the local mutts. I'd just cycled past the lake when one of them jumped out from behind the back of a car. I gave a roar to warn him off, but this had no effect. Instead the beast tried to take a bite out of my leg. I was wearing tracksuit bottoms and the dog ended up with a mouthful of cloth; he grazed my shin but not enough to make it bleed. I kicked him off and just peddled hard. The mutt ran after me barking loudly until the gap between us became sufficiently long enough that the animal lost interest. I felt a bit shook up. It was the first time that I ever really felt threatened by a dog. By the time I'd cycled a couple of kilometres the incident was almost forgotten about.

There are two roads that go through my housing estate; one for each side of the lake. It made sense to take the slightly longer route on the return journey so that I could avoid the crazy dog. I'd only made it half way down this road when a completely different dog took a lunge at me. The crafty fucker was waiting at one of the speed bumps; he obviously knew from experience that people needed to slow down here. This mutt had better aim than his friend, and he tried to sink his teeth right into the side of my foot. I was wearing sandals. This time there was a little bit of blood, but the skin wasn't fully broken. I kicked him off, but now I felt really shook up. Who gets bitten twice in one day by two different dogs?

I took the bike out again the next day, but my enthusiasm had suffered a major hit. I felt nervous every time a dog came anywhere near me. The animal from the first encounter took another lunge in my direction as I cycled past on my way out of the housing estate that morning. He didn't get near me, but I knew that he'd keep on trying until he struck gold. I spent the whole trip worrying about the return journey. That was my last outing on the bike; it now gathers dust at the side of the house. I'd noticed that some of the local cyclists carried sticks with them, but the idea of going around whacking dogs felt a bit unethical; surely there had to be a more humane way of getting exercise.

My cycling career had ended almost as soon as it had begun, and I still had the problem of getting ready for my first Muay Thai class. I fancied running in the neighbourhood even less now after my recent experiences. I found a novel solution. We have a path that goes right around our house. It only takes about 30 seconds to do a complete loop, but I reasoned that dizziness would be easier to deal with than rabies. Within a week I was managing to run like this for 30 minutes. My neighbours likely saw this behaviour as just more proof of the craziness of foreigners.

I mentioned my attempts to get fit enough to join a Muay Thai class on one of the online martial arts forums. I thought my plan made sense, but a few of the respondents to my post ridiculed me. When I thought about what they were saying I couldn't fault their logic. One guy nailed the problem with the words, "you don't get fit so you can go to the gym; you go to the gym to get fit". I realised that my plan was just procrastination; the time had come to bite the bullet and sign up for a Muay Thai class.

When I'm faced with any problem or query in life my automatic response is to Google it. This is what I did now to find a Muay Thai class. We had only recently moved to the outskirts of Bangkok from another part of Thailand. We needed to relocate because of my son's education, but I also liked the idea of all the conveniences associated with a big city. I'd lived in Bangkok a decade previously, but spent most of my time in bars. I'd no idea about Muay Thai clubs or where they were located in the capital. Before beginning my search I'd just assumed there would be a gym nearby, but that turned out to be wishful thinking.

My online search for a suitable Bangkok Muay Thai camp turned out to be a much bigger challenge than anticipated. There are plenty of these camps around, but none of them were near me. Travelling into central Bangkok seemed out of the question because the traffic would be a nightmare. Someone on one of the web forums mentioned Sitsongpeenong Gym. This place was located about 20km away and this seemed a reasonable distance to travel in the car.

The Sitsongpeenong website gave the impression of a professional training camp. The eight fighters showcased on the main page intimidated the hell out of me. A quick search showed that the youngest was only 13 years of age. I had no doubt that he would be able to kick me around the ring without breaking a sweat. I couldn't find any pictures of the foreign fighters at the camp, but I guessed that they too would be well out of my league. The idea of turning up at a place like that to train with such people seemed a bit ludicrous. Surely a real gym like this one wouldn't be the place for a flabby forty year old?

It had taken me such a long time to finally make the decision to learn Muay Thai. I didn't want to change my mind again. It would just be weak. It was more than that though. I also felt like I'd no longer any choice but to go ahead, I'd chosen my path and now all that could be done was follow it. I cursed myself for not choosing something a bit less physically demanding. I couldn't help once again thinking about how Tai Chi would have been a perfect martial art for somebody my age, and I already had some experience with it. I'd even come across a couple of Tai Chi classes in Bangkok during my search for a Muay Thai camp – maybe later.

So backing out now did not appear like an attractive option, but there could be some room for compromise. My biggest fear was looking foolish in front of a group of hardened Muay Thai students. I noticed that there were private classes, and this offered the perfect solution. I'd build up my fitness and learn some techniques before joining the regular class and facing other students. This would also mean that I'd be able to schedule these lessons at a convenient time.

In the few days before the class I made an effort to find out as much as I could about my new hobby. I bought a couple of books but these focused mostly on technique. It all looked interesting and impressive, but also a bit of a mystery. I made no attempt to practice any of the techniques in these texts. I sort of wanted to, but I reasoned that it might just end up confusing things. It would be better to learn directly from a teacher.

I also went online to search out some personal stories from people who had learnt Muay Thai. These were a lot more interesting for me to read. There were plenty of blogs focused on the combat system and most of the writers were passionate about their subject. I could feel myself being swept up by their enthusiasm. I started to feel like I had selected the right martial art for me.

Chapter 5

I RECEIVED AN EMAIL REPLY from Sitsongpeenong a few hours after sending my initial query. This is considered a speedy response by Thai standards so it impressed me. The author of the email was a guy called Tim. He assured me that my age wouldn't be a problem, and that they had people of all levels of experience training there. He also wrote that it would be possible to arrange private classes. I sent another email confirming that I would like to begin the following Saturday morning. He replied within minutes suggesting that we schedule my lesson for just after the morning session. This sounded fine to me. I'd finally done it. I felt both happy and nervous at the same time.

I sort of regretted not arranging a class for an earlier date. I now had five days to wait and worry about it. I began having nightmares. Each dream would be slightly different, but the core ingredients were the same. I'd turn up for my first class and somehow end up fighting in front of a cheering crowd. The applause wasn't there for my encouragement. This crowd was enjoying the spectacle of watching me being beaten to a pulp. I'd wake up with my heart pounding. I worried that this was my subconscious warning me of danger ahead. I tried to ignore this thought.

On the morning of the class I didn't feel too anxious at all – this calmness came as a pleasant surprise. It felt good to be finally following my dream. I'd just try one class. If it didn't work out then there would be no need for me to take things any further. I'd nothing to lose really. It was a lovely morning in Bangkok; more like a summer day back in Ireland where the heat isn't too excessive. The weather reflected my optimistic mood.

I'd actually driven the route to Sitsongpeenong the previous day; a sensible precaution given how difficult it can be to judge journey times in Bangkok. It took me 45 minutes due to a couple of traffic bottlenecks along the way. This time I gave myself an hour to make the journey. There turned out to be a lot less traffic on this trip. I got there in just 35 minutes. I didn't want to appear overly eager so I parked the car at the side of the road, just around the corner from the gym, and waited. A few of the local shop owners sent curious glances my way; one of them even came over to the car to see if I needed help. I pretended to use my mobile phone.

Sitsongpeenong Muay Thai Camp is located in the back of a small housing estate off Chalermprakiat Road. It is out on the east of the city not too far from Suvarnabhumi (pronounced suwan-a-pum) Airport. Sitsongpeenong is Thai for 'Two Brothers Gym'. The owners aren't really blood brothers; it is more an emotional thing. When you first turn into the estate there is a row of rundown shops and other business properties. There are nicer buildings once you get further inside, but a lot of land just sits empty. The

Camp is near the back of the estate at the end of a side road. It is a modern looking block-shaped building that looks well cared for. The top floor is where the actual training takes place.

IN MY EMAIL EXCHANGE WITH Tim I'd asked for advice on what to wear for my first lesson. Somehow the answer to this got missed in his email response. Rather than ask again I decided to just turn up in a pair of running shorts and a t-shirt. I didn't want to go out and buy a full Muay Thai kit for the first lesson. That might appear overeager. It would also be a waste of money if I decided not to continue after the first class. Oa was already making sarcastic comments about the unused bike; I didn't want to give her further ammunition.

I parked the car near the entrance to Sitsongpeenong. There were a couple of men in Muay Thai shorts outside eating at a table. They looked to be about my age so I judged them to be trainers. I got out of the car with the intention of asking them for directions, but they anticipated my question. One of them made a finger gesture that looked like an airplane going along the runway before taking off into the air. I guessed this to mean go through the hall and up the stairs.

I entered the building and became aware of the pleasant aroma of garlic and ginger. I spotted a modern looking restaurant area on my right hand side – nobody was in there. I went by a room with a TV and pool table. There were a couple of Thai teenagers inside, but they just ignored me. I noticed a pile of shoes in the corridor. I took this to mean that I needed to take off my footwear before going up the stairs. I kicked off my sandals before proceeding.

I did not see anyone else in the gym upstairs when I arrived. The first thing to hit me was another smell – something that reminded me of eucalyptus. I later found out that this odour came from Nam Muay; a lotion that Thai fighters use to help warm up their bodies. There were two boxing rings on the right hand side of the gym. Most of the left hand side was taken up with punch bags of different sizes. I also noticed an exercise bike and various weight lifting apparatus. The gym area had a pleasant breeze passing through it. The room had been built so that there were gaps in the walls where large windows might have normally been. I liked this design; it must save a fortune on air conditioning.

I spent a few minutes just sitting on the side of the ring. I didn't want to touch anything. I began to worry that maybe they weren't expecting me; perhaps there had been a mix-up with the time. My concerns were alleviated when a trainer appeared – the same man who had given me directions earlier. He introduced himself as Khru Jack – Khru is the Thai word for teacher. He smiled a lot and this put me at ease. I'd imagined a teacher who would be all business and professionalism. Jack was about my age and had the relaxed attitude that is the characteristic of so many Thais.

Khru Jack had a reasonable grasp of English. We were able to fill in any gaps of understanding with Thai. I could tell that he liked to speak my language so I tried to keep this as our lingua franca. Some people can get a bit insulted if you keep on reacting to their attempts to speak your language by replying in their language. It took me a few years of living in Thailand before I came to this realisation, but it makes a lot of sense. Nowadays if a Thai tries to engage me in English I'll reply to them in English. I have plenty of opportunities to speak Thai, but many of the local people do not get the same level of opportunity to practise my language.

The trainer told me to go and get changed. He looked a bit puzzled when I explained that this was it. He disappeared and came back with an old pair of Muay Thai shorts. I've always been a bit uncomfortable with the idea of wearing second hand clothes, but he wasn't leaving me much choice. This was my fault for not clarifying the situation before arriving. There was a toilet right beside the ring and he sent me in there to get changed. I just hoped that the last person wearing the shorts hadn't died in them.

Training began with warm up on the exercise bike. Khru Jack told me to keep going for 20 minutes, and then left me to it. I took it easy because I'd no idea about what was going to come afterwards – best save my energy. I did work up a little bit of a sweat, but the three days of my cycling career had paid dividends. Khru Jack didn't seem bothered one way or the other about my warm up efforts. He just sat on the side of the ring reading a Muay Thai magazine.

I shouted over to Khru Jack to let him know that I'd already cycled for 20 minutes. He waved me over, and began wrapping my hands in cloth. I'd only ever seen this done in boxing movies. He moved fast, but it was obvious that there was a technique to it. Jack began with a loop of the material around my wrist before wrapping the cloth in between my fingers; after each loop of the finger he would do another loop of the wrist. He then started wrapping the cloth around my fist until there was a good bit of padding on this part of my hand. He would keep getting me to open and close my fist so that he could get the wraps nice and snug. He finished off with a final loop around the wrist and finally used the Velcro at the end of the wraps to finish it off. He repeated the process on the other hand.

The teacher indicated for me to get into the ring. Memories of my recent nightmares came flooding back; maybe he really was expecting me to fight on the first day. Perhaps everyone had to do this before they could be allowed to learn Muay Thai? Some type of entrance test where the student proved his worthiness. I vaguely remembered a movie where that happened. It turned out that Khru Jack's expectations were nowhere near as high. He just told me to shadow box. I tried a few jabs and kicks; stuff I'd been practising on my bag at home.

I tried to impress Jack with my Kung Fu turning kick. I didn't realise that this was completely different from the turning kick used in Muay Thai. My strike ended at the imaginary centre line of a facing opponent; in Muay Thai you keep on going until your foot reaches the floor again.

Once Khru Jack had satisfactorily established that my fighting skills were shit he moved on to pad work. I'd already read on one of the Muay Thai blogs that working on the pads is a vital component of the training. It is the nearest you can get to fighting without a high risk of injury; although people do occasionally get hurt during pad training. The trainer uses these protective pads to defend against the attacks of the students. It takes a lot of skill and dexterity to manage this equipment correctly. I'd also read that if somebody is good with the pads it will automatically mean that they are a good fighter.

The trainer had pads on his forearms and a large belly pad across his abdominal area to absorb front kicks. He held up two pads on his left side at head level and ordered me to do a turning kick. He then moved the left forearm towards his face and ordered me to jab – or as he put it "yab". He did the same with the right forearm so that I could punch with the left. He then moved the two pads in an X shape above his abdominal area and ordered me to knee. I'd never really tried this move before, and it turned out to be a lot more difficult than I'd expected. The teacher told me to come up on the toes of the foot remaining on the ground and push forward with my hips. Not only was my knee to the pads embarrassingly weak, but I almost lost my balance every time. If Khru Jack had not managed to grab my arm on a couple of occasions I would have been arse down on the canvas.

Once the teacher had shown me the basics of pad work he picked up the pace. He began firing out instructions so that one technique followed another, "jab, jab, punch, right kick, jab, knee, jab, punch..." He had turned on a ring clock and this counted down from five minutes. When it reached zero it sounded an alarm, and then began a 30 second countdown which was the break in-between rounds.

I felt tired at the end of the first round, but pleased with my own performance. I felt like a real fighter. My strikes had made a satisfactory loud whack when they made contact with the pads; at least they sounded powerful. I didn't realise that this was only the first of five rounds, and that none of the rest of them would be as easy as the first. In-between each round Khru Jack would get me to drink ice-cool water. He would also pour a glass over my head. I don't usually like the feeling of cold water touching my skin, but as the rounds progressed I felt grateful for it. I wanted to remind him that this was only my first lesson; maybe nobody had told him. I kept on trying to slow down the action by asking him questions, but he didn't take the bait. I suspected the teacher of being some type of sadist; maybe his friendly smile had just been a ruse.

By the time we reached the end of round five I could barely stand up. The teacher pushed a glass of water towards my face, but I feebly pushed it away. The pace of my breathing meant that I would find it difficult to swallow. I wanted to vomit. Teacher Jack climbed out of the ring and motioned for me to do the same. I gratefully did so. I'd no idea about what came next, but it couldn't be any worse than what I'd just been through.

Khru Jack gave me a few seconds to get my breath back. I put my hands on my knees and bent forward. My breathing became slightly easier. I caught sight of myself in one of the gym mirrors. My face had gone almost purple – not a healthy look at all. My resolve for learning Muay Thai was beginning to wane when the teacher interrupted my thoughts with a timely pep talk. "You did very good. In six weeks no more ..." he mimicked my panting breath. He looked disapprovingly at my podgy stomach, and then slapped it. "In three months this will be all gone". Only one of his predictions turned out to be true.

The teacher brought me over to the area of the gym where the weights were kept. He ignored them and instead told me to lie down on a bench. I could tell by looking at the contraption that his motive here wasn't to give me a nice rest. I'd never used this type of bench, but I'd definitely seen one before. It was for doing sit-ups. I inwardly groaned because this is my least favourite exercise and I doubted that using a bench would make it any more pleasurable. I reluctantly followed instructions. I found it a bit awkward to position myself comfortably on the device. The part for lying on went down at an angle so that my head was closer to the ground than the rest of my body. I then had to hook my knees over one bar while tucking my feet under another bar slightly lower down.

When Khru Jack told me to do 100 sit-ups I thought I'd misheard him; perhaps his English wasn't so good after all. I asked for clarification in Thai which he happily gave to me. The most I've ever done is 50 sit-ups and that had been years before. I tend to avoid them. I hadn't even tried one sit-up since getting sober. There was no way that I could go from zero to 100 without building up to it; especially on a bench that had obviously been built to intensify the exercise. The teacher didn't share my pessimism. He shouted at me to start and then began counting my exertions. He would let me rest after each block of 20 for about thirty seconds. The first 50 sit-ups were surprisingly easy, but after 60 each of them felt torturous. I got my second wind at 95 because I could see the finish line.

My torturer said we were finished for the day. I felt relief. The class had been scheduled for one hour, but we had already gone 20 minutes over. I couldn't have done one more exercise. I felt exhausted, but also joyful at the same time. I'd made it to the end of my first Muay Thai class. I asked Khru Jack if he'd ever trained anyone else at my level of fitness, but he reassured me that I was not the worst. Maybe he just said this out of kindness but I didn't care. I felt good. He told me to go get a shower. I didn't have a towel, so I just threw water over myself and put my clothes on without drying off. I limped back out to my car.

I continued to feel good as I drove home from my first Muay Thai lesson. My performance at the gym had been far from impressive, but I had to start somewhere. At least I now knew that I could make it through a class. I thought about the teacher's claim that after six weeks it would all become a lot easier. That made sense, but I worried that my week long gaps between classes would slow down the acclimatisation process. I'd need to train a lot harder at home.

I couldn't remember ever having pushed myself physically as hard as I had during those five rounds on the pads. I would not have believed that someone with my level of fitness would be capable of keeping up that pace. I'd underestimated my potential; something I do a lot. I suspect that it is a problem for most people. The danger with always setting the bar low is that it reduces the likelihood of finding real success and happiness in life.

It had been this lack of belief in my own abilities that kept me from taking up Muay Thai until middle age. I remember during my mid-twenties I'd considered attending a kickboxing class. I dismissed the idea then because of my age. I decided to learn Tai Chi instead. I do not regret one bit the decision to learn that less physically demanding martial art, but I did sometimes feel like I'd settled for second best.

I remember that for our Sunday Tai Chi class we would share the gym with another group who were learning Kung Fu. They would be doing all sorts of hard physical stuff, but I'd be there moving like a snail through the Tai Chi form. I could see that these other martial artists saw us Tai Chi people as a bit of a joke. I would treacherously feel the same way myself sometimes. I yearned to be with this other group, but I just didn't think that I was capable. Now here I was 15 years later doing one of the most intense martial arts on the planet.

I try to avoid getting caught in the 'what if' mode of thinking. Such mental voyages are just a waste of time. For better or worse I'm stuck with the results of the decisions I made in the past. Luckily for me I happen to really like my life now. If things didn't happen exactly as they did I wouldn't be where I am. I like where I am.

People are surprised, or even annoyed, when I tell them that I don't regret my alcoholic past. It is a bit of a bizarre claim to make I suppose. After all, how could I not feel ashamed of all those wasted years and the people I hurt along the way? I do feel bad about the damage done; I'm not some type of psychopath after all. I've just reached a point in my life where I'm at peace with my past; it was part of the journey

I like to think of alcoholism as a type of training program. Those who successfully graduate from the course learn some invaluable lessons about life. The training is hard. Addiction gives people a stark choice; you either become a better person or you die. Those who make it out of addiction are forced on a journey of self-improvement. This is the only way that they can put a safe distance between themselves and a life of substance abuse. It is like nature is forcing us to do the things that will help us achieve real happiness in life. That isn't a bad thing at all. You don't have to be an addict for your life to be shitty. The people I feel most sorry for are those who just accept a miserable life. Things just never get bad enough that they are forced into making a change.

I completely disagree when people make the claim that 'a leopard can't change its spots' – that's just negative bullshit usually offered by individuals who have a limited imagination. People can completely turn their lives around – I did. It is true that change is hard. That is because there is so much comfort in the familiar; even when the familiar is ruining your life. I suppose some of us respond better to pain than others; we get the message and change our ways. The unfortunate ones have so much tolerance for pain that it kills them. I have met so many addicts like that; all they had to do to end their addiction was to take a leap of faith into the unknown but instead they just stubbornly hung onto their misery until it killed them.

Their wasted life makes me feel angry and sad. This is why the words, 'a leopard can't change its spots' irritates me so much. That type of thinking gets people killed.

Discomfort can be nature's attempt at telling us we have lost our way. The more we insist in following this wrong path the greater our pain. The upside is that when we finally do get back on track we experience a great deal of joy – it is like the universe is congratulating us for our good work. I sort of felt this way now. There had been a push towards learning Muay Thai for years, but I kept on resisting. I'd now stopped resisting so the flow could take me where I needed to be. I realise that talk about the 'universe congratulating me' must sound like wishy-washy bullshit to a lot of people. I sometimes feel the same way. I just can't think of a better explanation.

Chapter 6

IT TOOK ME THREE DAYS to recover from that first Muay Thai session. The real damage had come from the sit-ups; that exertion had left a band of burning pain across my stomach area. My abdominal muscles were so uncomfortable that I could hardly sleep the first night. I limped around the house like an old man. Oa felt that this should be enough to convince me of the foolishness of attempting such an extreme activity, but I didn't mind the pain. I'd never expected it to be easy. My main worry had been that I wouldn't be able to make it through even one class. Despite feeling like a bit of a physical wreck it had been mission accomplished.

I added the new moves I'd picked up in my first class to my home exercise regime. Using my knee as a weapon was new to me, and it just felt awkward. I read somewhere online that practicing any technique a few thousand times builds up muscle memory; this means that the movements become automatic. Mastering the knee strike felt important; Muay Thai fighters are famous for using this particular part of the body to devastating effect. So I came up with the ambitious plan of doing 100 knee strikes on the bag each day. When I attempted this the first time I only made it to thirty. I gave up because the skin on my right knee began to peel away. I settled on a more modest regime of twenty knees on the bag per session. I would increase the amount once my skin had toughened up a bit.

Khru Jack had shown me a new way of doing the roundhouse kick/turning kick. This is probably the most effective technique in Muay Thai; when it is on target it is like hitting the opponent with a baseball bat. Almost all the most famous Muay Thai knockouts involve this strike. Other martial arts use the turning kick but no other style is as devastatingly effective with it. In Kung Fu I'd learnt to just snap this type of kick out, but this is not the way things are done in Thailand. Instead you use the hips and abdominal muscles to create momentum and you keep turning until you hit something. Another big difference is that you need to come up on the ball of the foot and pivot. This all meant that my previous experience with the roundhouse kick didn't give me any advantage; if anything it made it harder because I had to unlearn old habits.

I'd felt proud of my ability to still be able to do a reasonable Kung fu turning kick despite how out of shape I'd become. I had even insisted that Oa and my son Timmy come out to see me do this technique on the bag the week before. This new way of doing a roundhouse kick proved to be a huge challenge for me. I found it difficult to come up on the ball of the foot without losing my balance. Practising without a target turned out to be particularly hard because I'd need to move in a 180 degree spin. If I did this more than a couple of times I'd feel dizzy. I also tended to fall down a lot. I found it much easier to do the Muay Thai roundhouse on the bag because this stopped the momentum and prevented the dizziness.

I began focusing on the more technical Muay Thai videos on YouTube. Some of the tutorials were quite good, but there were conflicting explanations of how the actions should be performed. I decided to not get too caught up in the details but just focus on the general movement I was trying to imitate. This approach had worked for me when learning Tai Chi. I'd first learn a square version of the form with the emphasis on just remembering the overall pattern. Once I'd become comfortable with this the object would then be to focus more closely on the individual techniques – I could do that in class under the guidance of a teacher. This way the techniques would move from square and clunky to round and smooth. Apparently this is similar to how a sculptor works; they start off with a lump of shapeless rock, but slowly over time they chip away at it until it begins to resemble something more appealing to the eye.

The lesson at Sitsongpeenong had not been my first encounter with Muay Thai. Twenty-five years before I'd attended a weekend seminar in Dublin with Master Sken; a teacher who is credited as being one of the first to introduce the Thai martial arts into Europe. He had once been a champion fighter and managed to retire undefeated. In the '70s he moved to the UK where he developed a reputation as a skilled teacher. He'd agreed to visit us in Ireland to introduce us to the combat system. He was not only to be the first Muay Thai fighter I met, but also the first Thai person.

Master Sken's visit had been organised by the Irish Lau Gar Kung Fu Association. They had decided to hold the event in my local gym. I lived in a small village on the outskirts of Dublin, in a place called Shankill, and we didn't receive many visiting foreign dignitaries. His arrival meant a big deal for those of us in the local martial arts community. I had to go to this event. Luckily I didn't have to pester my father too hard to get the admission fee; this was something he did not want to miss out on either.

My memories of those two days with Master Sken are a bit vague – it is all so long ago. He did give a demonstration at the start of the seminar, and this left a lasting impression on me. At one point he launched into a continuous movement of turning and spinning kicks; knocking cans off people's head as he went. This in itself wasn't anything that special; I'd seen other martial artists do similar feats. The thing that made it exceptional was the grace of his movements. I could see that he had perfect control over every muscle in his body; he moved like an exotic animal. He shadow boxed and the power of his strikes caused vibrations in the air. I'd never seen anything quite like it before.

I got to experience the strength of Master Sken's kicks for myself on the second day. He picked me as a partner to demonstrate a roundhouse kick to the thigh. My job was simply to stand there in fighting stance while he hit me. He only used a little bit of power, but it was like being struck with an iron bar. I dreaded to think what it must have been like to be up against him in the ring when he wasn't holding back. My thigh felt completely numb; I could barely stand. This numbness couldn't have lasted more than 30 seconds, but if it had been a real fight I would have been defenceless.

I developed a lot of respect for Muay Thai because of Master Sken's seminar. Not enough to make me want to take up this martial art though; I doubt this would have been even possible at the time anyway. Now there are many Muay Thai clubs in Ireland but back in the '80s I don't think there were any. On the last day we got to watch some videos of his Muay Thai fights, and it just appeared so savage. It looked like the fighters were trying to kill each other using any possible means; compared to this Western boxing looked tame. I got flustered by light sparring so full-contact Muay Thai would be well out of my league. When the seminar ended I didn't expect to have any further contact with this Thai martial art – funny how life turns out.

Chapter 7

I WAS LOOKING FORWARD TO my next lesson at Sitsongpeenong. I figured that one of the reasons why the first session had been so physically demanding was that I'd been overenthusiastic. I decided that this time I'd hold back a bit; I'd pace myself better. These were private lessons, after all, and 'he who pays the piper gets to call the tune', as they say. I'd yet to figure out that Khru Jack only marched to his own tune.

My plan to preserve energy at the next lesson fell apart at the first hurdle. When Khru Jack told me to warm up on the stationary bike I expected a repeat performance of the week before but this time he didn't just leave me alone to work at my own pace. He sat down on the sit-up bench right beside me. I'd only been riding for a little over a minute when he became fed up with my laid back approach. He leaned over and changed the settings so that the bike mimicked much tougher terrain. It now felt like cycling uphill. He kept shouting, "reow, reow" to motivate me to pick up the pace. After ten minutes the sweat began to drip off my body. The back of my legs felt like they were going to cramp. I just lowered my head towards the control panel and kept on pedalling.

When I told Khru Jack that the 20 minutes on the bike were up he looked at me suspiciously. I wasn't lying, but his disapproving look encouraged me to keep pedalling for an additional five minutes. My legs felt unsteady as I climbed off the bike. I expected to be able to sit down while the teacher put on the hand wraps, but instead he got me to run around the gym for ten minutes. When he did get around to putting the wraps on my hands he moved like a demon; I'd barely put my arse down on the side of the ring when he was finished. It was like he somehow knew about my intention to take it easy and now wanted to punish me for it.

The five rounds on the pads were relentless. I vaguely worried that the pace could kill me but near the end I was too tired to care. The idea of just giving up didn't enter my thinking. I'd recently read a book about Bruce Lee called *The Art of Expressing the Human Body* written by John Little. A lot of the text is devoted to different exercise regimes, but I preferred the introductory chapters where the focus was on Lee's philosophy for life. I liked one story in particular. It described how this Kung Fu legend had been out running with one of his students. Keeping up the pace with a fitness freak like Bruce Lee must have been difficult so it is understandable that his protégé began to struggle. The student complained that he needed to stop or he would die. Lee replied that it would be better to die than to give up. This idea carried me through those five rounds with Khru Jack. A couple of times I again tried to slow down the pace by asking questions, but I might as well not have bothered. After a couple of rounds I felt too tired to ask questions anyway. I just wanted the ordeal to end. I felt strangely elated at the end of the fifth round. I knew that we were over the toughest part of the lesson.

My attempt to set the pace of the second lesson had failed miserably. I did manage to snatch one last minute victory while doing the sit-ups. Khru Jack was chatting with one of the other trainers; I doubted that even he could talk and count my reps at the same time. I stopped at 80 instead of going to 100 as ordered. I then slipped off to the showers before he could ask me to do anything else. It turned out to be a shallow victory because of guilt – after all I was only cheating myself.

I found Khru Jack waiting downstairs for me after my shower; he had one of the foreign students with him; a young clean-cut guy called Bobby who came from the United States. He looked to be in his late teens or early twenties. There were brief introductions before the two of them climbed into the back of my car. I'd no idea where they wanted to go. I asked Khru Jack but he just smiled and waved his finger forward. I'd no problem taking them wherever they needed to go within reasonable distance. I'd not yet had an opportunity to speak with any of the other foreigners training at Sitsongpeenong so I welcomed the opportunity. I had lots of questions.

Bobby had just finished two months training at Sitsongpeenong. He'd fought a few days previously and lost. The fight had only lasted two rounds, but it had been gruelling; he had to be carried out of the ring at the end. He'd recovered fast except for his left knee which still remained swollen and sore. It had been his first fight, and he had no intention of getting back in the ring again anytime soon. He asked if I'd fought yet; I took it as a compliment that he would even consider it possible. Bobby didn't regret fighting, and he urged me to do it at least once. He talked about his experience at the camp in a way that left me in no doubt that it had all been life changing. I fired questions at Bobby as if he were a contestant on a quiz show.

I wanted to know more about the experience of learning Muay Thai full-time. I found training for one hour once a week such a challenge yet these guys were managing five hours or more each day for six days a week. Bobby admitted that it had been hard in the beginning. During the first week he'd become ill as his body adapted to the intensity of the training. He'd also picked up plenty of injuries over the course of the two months. It had all been worth it because he had managed to reach such a high level of fitness and his Muay Thai technique had improved so much. The more he talked the more I envied him the experience.

WHEN WE ARRIVED AT THE main road Khru Jack directed me to pull over to the pavement. This would be as far as my passengers would be going; they wanted to visit the nearby Carrefour supermarket. I still had questions for Bobby queued up on my tongue so I sort of felt disappointed that the journey ended so soon. I can go weeks without talking to somebody who is a native English speaker so I like to make the most of these opportunities.

The second lesson had been physically more intense than the first, but the after-effects were a lot less. This time I only limped around the house for one day instead of three. Over the next few weeks my body acclimatised. I continued to find the class a huge challenge, but my recovery time afterwards decreased. The private lesson became something to look forward to each Saturday.

Chapter 8

TURNING UP TO A MARTIAL arts class isn't going to sound like such a big achievement to most people. It's not exactly climbing Mount Everest is it? When I consider where I've come from it does seem like a big deal to me. For so much of my life I'd been a waster. Five years before this I'd been ready to die. I'd finally hit rock bottom after two decades of alcohol abuse. At the time I lived in a Thai village with a damaged liver and a death wish. I'd become convinced that life would never get any better and maybe the best thing would be just to drink myself to death. It felt like I'd run out of options. I'd hit my first rehab at 20 years of age and it felt like I'd tried every addiction treatment program the West had to offer. I'd given up all hope of there ever being a cure that would work for me. It was then that I heard about a Thai temple called Thamkrabok.

I talk about my fall into addiction and how I finally escaped in my first book *Dead Drunk*. I don't want to go back over old ground too much here, but suffice to say I was in bad shape back then. I remember one day in Chiang Mai watching Muay Thai on the TV in a bar. I turned around to my newest drinking buddy and told him how I'd love to learn that fighting art. He looked at me with pity in his eyes. I might as well have told him that I wanted to put the moon on a stick. Who was I kidding? The only exercise I managed these days was the shaking that my body went through before my first drink in the morning.

When I gave up alcohol at Thamkrabok detox temple I only hoped for the pain to stop. I didn't feel I deserved even that. Since going through that program back in June 2006 my life has been completely turned around – there is no comparison. I'm married to a beautiful wife who stuck with me through the final days of my addiction. My childhood dream of being a writer is a reality. My wonderful son has given new meaning to my life. He has never seen me drunk, and it is my promise that he never will. The real miracle is that I feel so mentally at peace a lot of the time – I used to be such a mental wreck. Believe me I do have my bad days, but for the most part I'm happy and that is not something I would have believed possible a few years ago.

I'm a late bloomer and there's nothing wrong with that. I'm still young enough to get plenty of enjoyment out of life. Most of the limitations associated with age are things we put on ourselves anyway. They say that the peak of physical fitness occurs in the early twenties, but that certainly wasn't the case with me – I was a wreck back then. This means that my physical peak is probably still ahead of me in middle age.

I do need to be realistic though. I'm not going to be able to take back up martial arts where I left it off. For one thing my body has changed a great deal since then. I've also got too many responsibilities to lose myself in the practice like I was able to in my teens. It is not all bad news. In some ways I have advantages over my younger self. I'm mentally tougher, and my body is stronger too.

A few months before beginning my training at Sitsongpeenong I'd read a book by Sang H. Kim called *Martial Arts after 40*. I found this manual to be useful even though at times the content left me feeling gloomy; a reminder that my body could no longer do the things that it once could. This was the first time I'd ever read anything aimed at the 'over forties crowd' and it will probably be my last – not that I've anything against this particular title. Overall the book left a positive impression. It added weight to my assumption that I could do something like Muay Thai no matter what my age. I might not experience it the exact same way as young people, but that didn't have to mean it would be an inferior experience.

LEARNING MARTIAL ARTS IS UNFINISHED business for me. I lost this passion to addiction so it just feels right that I should reclaim it now that I'm sober. To be honest, I'm not completely sure there is anything particularly special about my yearning to learn a combat system. Maybe if I'd been interested in a different activity during my formative years I'd want to do that now. I should count myself lucky then that my earlier passion had not been for Irish dancing; finding a class in Thailand would be a complete nightmare. Ultimately it probably does not matter what activities we are drawn to; what is important is how we relate to them.

Bad things happened to me during my years of

addiction, but it wasn't always the lowest points that hurt me the most. One event that sticks in my mind happened in the Thai beach resort of Pattaya. Anyone who has been there will know that it is a drinker's paradise; thousands of bars selling cheap alcohol – they call it 'Sin City'. I loved it there. Pattaya is the place most responsible for giving Thailand the reputation as a destination for sex tourists but for me the main attraction would be the opportunities for drunkenness.

Oa was still only my girlfriend back then. We were living in rural Phitsanulok, but I'd talked her into accompanying me to Pattaya. A weekend of watching me get drunk – how could she resist? It was early in the evening and we were sitting in a British bar. There were a couple of lads at the table next to us, and I decided to invite myself into their conversation. I'd already been living in Thailand a few years by then, and I liked to impress strangers with my local knowledge. I pulled my chair over to their table; leaving Oa to sit staring into space.

It turned out that these English guys were in Thailand to learn Muay Thai. I'd struck conversational gold. I began telling them my 'poor me' story about how I'd lost martial arts to the demon drink. They listened patiently enough, but I could tell they weren't impressed. They were joined by another guy in his forties who owned his own martial arts gym in Northeast Thailand. I tried to impress him with my 20 year old stories of former Kung Fu glory, but he wasn't having any of it. He looked at me as if I was complete vermin and said, "fuck off pisshead". His friends laughed at this, and I felt completely pathetic as I moved the chair back to my own table. I turned back to Oa and tried to act as if I hadn't just been humiliated in public.

Being told to "fuck off" by a complete stranger could be described as minor shit when compared to a lot of other things that happened to me in bars over the years. It just hurt more because they were martial artists. I needed them to accept me as one of their tribe. I can't remember exactly what was going through my head at the time, but I'd be surprised if I wasn't imagining that these people could save me. Instead of telling me to fuck off I'd wanted that martial arts teacher to take me under his wing. Sort of like in the movie *The Karate Kid* – instead this time it would be the Karate Middle Aged Drunk.

I suppose I can't blame those guys for being so rude that day. If I had been stuck listening to some drunken idiot ramble on incoherently I would have felt tempted to do the same – I probably would have been more diplomatic about it though. I wasn't a bad person back then; just someone a bit out of control. I'm not completely convinced by the arguments that alcoholism is a disease, but it is certainly not a life that people adopt intentionally.

Chapter 9

KHRU JACK SAT WAITING OUTSIDE when I arrived for my next lesson. He came over to the car even before I'd had a chance to open the door. He was accompanied by a younger Thai man. Jack explained how he was too busy that day, and needed to pass over the responsibility for my instruction to this other teacher. I felt a bit excited at the prospect but also a little bit worried. What if this younger guy tried to push me harder than Khru Jack? Mind you, I couldn't really imagine how that would be possible.

I liked Khru Ton right away. He had a nice easy manner about him and a bit of a twinkle in his eye. I could tell that he liked to laugh a lot. He acted a bit hesitant towards me at first, but once he realised my Thai language skills were reasonable he became quite chatty. We walked upstairs together to the gym. I felt eager to get the session going; I'd promised Oa and Timmy that I'd take them out shopping when I got back. Khru Ton didn't seem to be in any rush to begin; he just continued asking questions about my life. In the end I just hopped on the bike to warm up even without him suggesting it. I cycled at a leisurely pace for 20 minutes and Khru Ton didn't seem to mind in the slightest.

After the warm up it was straight into the ring for some pad work. Khru Ton had a different teaching style to Jack. He put a lot more emphasis on performing the technique correctly. I liked this about him. I often felt like Jack allowed bad technique to slide just to keep me moving. I also found Khru Ton to be far more receptive to questions. If I asked him to explain something he would stop and show me. Of course this was highly advantageous for me because it meant that I could slow the action down every time I felt too tired. I wasn't getting as tough a workout as I would under Khru Jack, but learning so much made up for that.

One thing that unsettled me with Khru Ton's method for doing the pads was how he would attack me out of nowhere. Khru Jack would always shout at me to keep my guard up high, but this other teacher had a more direct approach. Every time he noticed a gap in my defences he would attack it; this kept me on my toes and meant that the session became far more of a technical challenge. Every time he launched into an attack I would become flustered and just tuck my head under my arms – this is called turtling up and it is far from a winning strategy.

Khru Ton shared some of his life story with me. Apparently his family had been against the idea of him learning Muay Thai. This meant that he had to train in secret as a youngster, and eventually ran away from home to follow his dreams. I really admired his determination. I doubt that I would have been able to do the same – in fact I know I wouldn't. Khru Ton had achieved success as a fighter and now he had secured a job as a trainer in one of the top Muay Thai camps in Thailand.

I've always tended to view fighters as hard nuts with psychopathic tendencies. I sort of imagined that to be a good Muay Thai fighter you had to be completely macho and aggressive. Khru Ton appeared to be a gentle sort of bloke, and I found it hard to imagine him kicking the shit out of somebody else. The same thing could be said about Khru Jack as well. Obviously I had no real idea about what drove fighters to do what they do.

The next time I returned to Sitsongpeenong I was back training with Khru Jack. I did get a couple more private lessons with Khru Ton; I would have liked more. I enjoyed both of these trainers' teaching styles for different reasons. I always left a session with Jack feeling like I'd pushed my body to the limit. When I finished a session with Khru Ton I would have more of a feeling that I'd learnt something new.

Chapter 10

I KNEW THAT JUST ONE Muay Thai session per week wasn't much at all. I would need to do a lot more than this if I wanted to see progress. The fear of suffering during the Saturday session encouraged me to be more physically active during the week. I would train every evening for half an hour. I'd hoped to be able to do more than this, but I'd just feel so exhausted after a day staring at the computer. I'm lucky enough to make my living from doing a job I love, but writing is physically and mentally draining – especially doing it for ten hours a day or more.

When I began mentioning to people that I'd taken up Muay Thai lessons the usual response would be a bit of negativity. People just felt this type of activity was far too dangerous; especially for someone at my age and lack of experience. I could see where they were coming from, but doubted that it could be any more dangerous than sitting at my desk all day. Since giving up teaching to become a full-time writer I'd moved from one injury to the next. The first thing to be affected was my eyesight, but every week there seems to be a new part of my body experiencing discomfort.

It turns out that sitting down at a desk all day is one of the most dangerous things you can do – more dangerous than any martial art. It can take years off the human lifespan. I've no problem accepting this claim, because I've seen for myself how damaging this type of work can be. Forget about Alaskan crab fishing; if you want a dangerous job just sit at your desk all day. It felt like I'd aged physically about a decade in one year. The body is fantastic at adapting to whatever it is we are doing; even if it means killing us in the process. I was turning into some type of computer slug.

Writing is more than a job to me. I'd still be doing it even without a pay check. I loved working as a nurse, but it just wasn't something I could imagine doing for the rest of my life. I also had good days working as an English teacher in Thailand but I never felt comfortable in that role so giving that up came as a bit of a relief – if I'm honest. It's different with writing; I've no urge to work at anything else. I'll be happy to die at my desk. I'm so grateful to have finally found a job that I know is right for me. There is nothing glamorous about the writing life, the reality of it would probably seem boring to most sane people, but it just suits me fine. The only downside is the speed at which my health is deteriorating. When I wrote just now that I'd be 'happy to die at my desk' I pictured a scene where I'm at least 80 years old. Unless I can stop the deterioration to my health this death scene could occur a lot sooner.

Half an hour of exercise a day isn't enough for someone who sits around so much of the time, but of course it is better than no exercise. I've a poor track record with the 'all or nothing' approach, I end up achieving nothing. This time I'd try a different strategy. Starting off slowly can lead to greater things because at least it gets me into the habit of doing exercise regularly. If I could encourage my body to develop a thirst for the feel-good hormones that are produced by intense physical effort it would just get easier after that. I hoped that exercise would become something that I want to do and not just something that I felt I should be doing.

I felt disappointed because this new Muay Thai exercise routine wasn't having much of an impact on my body weight. I'd been going to lessons for over two months, but I'd actually put on a couple of kilograms. Khru Jack had promised me at the first lesson that he'd get my weight down. He took my failure to lose weight personally. He would push me harder and harder each week. I worried that unless my weight started to fall he would exercise me to death. Of course it wasn't the fault of the trainer or Muay Thai that my podgy stomach continued to expand. This activity meant that I burnt an extra couple of thousand calories per week, but I consumed about four thousand calories more than I needed during that same time period.

The event that gave me the needed push to lose weight occurred while on a day out with my wife and son at Funarium, a children's indoor play area in central Bangkok. Sunday is family day in our house, and we try to go somewhere that Timmy will enjoy. It also gives me a break from my work. The thing I like most about Funarium is that there is plenty to keep kids entertained, but also somewhere for me to sit with a coffee and read a book.

The centrepiece of Funarium is a multi-storey play structure where kids can climb, slide, and just generally go wild. My son lacked the confidence to tackle such a monster by himself, but usually felt happy with my wife as his playmate. This setup suited me fine. As far as I'm concerned Sunday is my day off. I've done my bit by bringing them somewhere entertaining; it is up to them to make the most of it. This deal didn't suit my son on this particular day; he guilt-tripped me into accompanying him. Oa disappeared before I could think of a good excuse to get out of it.

Timmy shot off like a demented monkey, and it was all I could do to keep up with him. With all the climbing and sliding I felt exhausted after just a few minutes. I didn't mind because I could see how much my son was enjoying it. We were on the top of the structure when I came to a pole that we were meant to climb across. There were plenty of ropes on each side to make sure that nobody would fall. A sign beside this bridge warned of an 80kg maximum load; when I'd last weighed myself I'd been 84kg.

If we had been back in Europe I might have been tempted to cross this bar. I knew that they usually left a huge margin of error for safety reasons and out of the fear of being sued. I couldn't be sure that the same leeway would exist with a maximum load in Thailand – perhaps they didn't factor in allowances for human stupidity. Maybe if I walked across the whole structure would come tumbling down. I could imagine the newspaper headlines, 'Scores of Kids Killed When Fatty Collapses Bangkok Play Structure.' No doubt I'd get over the embarrassment, but the guilt would be harder to deal with.

A queue began to form behind me; impatient

youngsters who just wanted me out of their way. Timmy waited on the other side of the bar with a confused look on his face. I could feel my face going red as I struggled to think of a way out of my predicament. The only option open to me was retreat. I called my son back, but he wasn't having any of it. I'd no choice but to move backwards as kids tried to climb over me. It turned out to be a real squeeze, but I somehow managed to get back down to the lower level. I began to experience panic because Timmy was still left somewhere up above me. I knew he couldn't get into too much trouble, but he would be upset because I'd just abandoned him. I felt fat and stupid because of my powerlessness to take care of my son. I felt such relief when I saw him coming shooting out of a loopy-loop slide – thankfully he didn't appear too fazed by my disappearance.

It turned out to be an enjoyable day at Funarium, but the experience on the bar bridge continued to play on my mind. It had been the first time I couldn't do something because of my weight. I knew my size would be considered pretty standard for people back in the West, but it is not so easy to blend in if you are overweight in Thailand. The heat makes it impossible to hide a porky stomach under layers of clothing. Thai people tend to be slim, and this makes me more self-conscious of my own weight.

By the time we got home that evening I'd entered a real funk. I felt angry because I'd allowed my weight to deteriorate so badly. I'd fought so hard to escape the unhealthy life of the alcoholic yet here I was following a new path to an early grave. This is not how I wanted to live. I made a vow there and then to get my weight down as quickly as possible and never again allow it to climb higher than 75kg.

I knew that I could lose the weight, but this wasn't going to be enough. I wanted to keep it off. That would involve lifestyle changes and not temporary fixes. Practicing Muay Thai every day would help me stay in shape, but it wouldn't be enough to fix my weight problems. I'd need to make changes to my diet as well. I knew that by reducing my calorie intake I'd be able to bring my weight down to an acceptable level within a couple of months – but then what? Reducing calories requires a conscious effort and eventually I would run out of steam. I didn't want a future of rollercoaster body weight. One possible solution to my weight problems involved meditation. On a few occasions I'd recommended mindful eating to other people, but I'd never got around to trying it myself.

Chapter 11

KUNG FU TRAINING INTRODUCED ME to the practice of meditation, and it has been a part of my life ever since. Even during some of the worst days of my alcohol addiction I would attempt to meditate; of course my regular intoxication meant I'd get zero benefit from this. I did have some success using mindfulness techniques to help me deal with cravings. I even spent one month meditating in a Thai temple; I didn't manage to quit alcohol right away after this, but it did nudge me in the right direction. It wasn't until I finally stopped drinking that I really began to benefit from the practice. It is now a key component of my sobriety. I do not need any convincing about the power of meditation, and this is why the idea of mindful eating appeals to me so much.

I suppose when most people hear the word 'meditation' they picture somebody sitting cross legged and chanting 'Om'. What many of us fail to realise is that meditation does not have to be anything special. Just walking in nature and admiring the scenery can be a form of meditation; so can playing a musical instrument or focusing intently on the job at hand. Even Muay Thai is a form of meditation if it is done with focus. The majority of people meditate at least occasionally but most of us would not give it that label; it is just something we do naturally.

Sometimes when I mention meditation to people they try to change the subject. They may even make an excuse to escape my company altogether – most likely assuming that I'm some type of religious fanatic. I suppose it is hard for people who don't meditate as a formal practice to understand what it is all about. For me it is a way to keep my brain in good physical shape.

When I stop meditating my mental state starts to deteriorate; I become far more susceptible to negative thinking. I'm not saying that I turn into some type of nutcase, but there is a definite decline in my mental processes. There is also this feeling of sluggishness that develops in my brain if I miss a few days of meditation. I only really notice this when I start to meditate again. As soon as I get back to the practice after a break it is like dipping my brain into a lovely relaxing warm bath – that is the best way that I can describe it. The wonders of meditation amaze me. I don't believe that humans have even touched the surface of the possibilities of this practice.

I'd already experimented with being mindful while training in Muay Thai and the results were impressive. It is certainly a great improvement on just going through the motions. I've an awful habit of daydreaming in the midst of training. I'd be doing the pads with Khru Jack while at the same time planning my evening meal or thinking about my next work assignment. My lack of concentration meant that I'd only been hitting the pads half-heartedly and paying no attention to the person holding them. The fact that I'm not really there must have been obvious because this is usually the time when Khru Jack decided to test my defences. He usually sends some punches or kicks my way, and I'd be too lost in a daydream to stop them. The best I can do is put up a half-hearted defence after the strike has landed. I'd be rewarded for my efforts with Jack shouting "mai dee" – no good.

The scary thing is that it is just so easy for me to slip into this mindless state – most people I speak to have the same problem. This is something that I have to constantly fight against, and 99% of the time I fail miserably. I'm always daydreaming and thinking about things that have no real connection with what is going on in my life now. I used to think that this was just my temperament as a writer, but that was just wishful thinking. I'm far more effective at writing when my mind isn't galloping about the place like a wild horse. In simple terms meditation can be described as just trying to escape this mindless state, and I don't have to be sitting on a cushion to do that.

Being mindful while doing Muay Thai makes a huge difference. I later found that a certain level of mindfulness comes naturally during sparring. The body goes on high alert so focus is increased; daydreaming while sparring would almost certainly lead to a lot of pain. There is not a naturally high level of mindfulness when doing pads because the level of threat is much lower – especially when the teacher isn't making the workout challenging enough. I tended to be more mindful when training with Khru Ton because he would be more likely to launch an attack against me.

This is when being deliberately mindful can be most effective.

I found that being mindful just makes the training more pleasurable. I even feel less exhausted when doing the pads mindfully. This is because much of the discomfort comes from negative mental chatter. The Buddha explained this with the story of the two arrows. When we are heedless it doubles our suffering; it is like being hit with two arrows instead of just one. The pain of what we are doing is increased unnecessarily as the mind experiences a hissy fit. When I'm not focused the aversion that arises in my mind is tougher to deal with than the actual discomfort in the body. All the time my mind is going, "I don't like this" and this magnifies any tiredness or pain.

When I'm mindful of the discomfort of the training it is so much easier to handle. My thinking isn't in panic mode so the discomfort is an irritation rather than a major source of concern – I can calmly remind myself that the discomfort won't last forever. If I'm daydreaming I can slip into this panic mode without even realising what is going on.

I'd read a few personal accounts of how mindful eating worked well for weight management. It made perfect sense to me. The thing that most appealed to me was that it wasn't just another fad diet. This involved a whole new approach for dealing with food. It would be something that once adopted would become a permanent part of my life. I also liked that it created another use for my existing meditation practice. As an added bonus it would also increase my general mindfulness level, and this would improve other areas of my life too. I really do believe that happiness is related to the extent that we can live in the moment.

Mindful eating simply means becoming more aware of food, and its effects on the body. Like a lot of other people I've developed the bad habit of just shoving things in my mouth without really thinking about it too much. I also eat fast and this means that my stomach doesn't get a chance to register when I'm full. Mindful eating not only involves an increased awareness about the actual eating process, but also the reasons why I'm eating in the first place. I tend to eat a lot when I'm tired, stressed, or feeling down, but this has nothing to do with hunger. Comfort eating is a bit of a misnomer because the only benefit from this activity, that I can see, is the accumulation of fat – not much of a benefit unless you're an Eskimo with no money for clothes.

Some of the mindful eating experts suggest that one of the reasons why we eat so much is that our food fails to satisfy us mentally. When I gobble down food my senses don't get a chance to appreciate what is going on. I'm usually focused on the computer screen so I don't even look at what I'm putting into my mouth most of the time. This failure to appreciate food means that I'm mentally unsatisfied at the end of a meal – my mind still feels hunger for the taste and other sensations connected to eating. My body has been given more fuel, but my mind didn't even get a chance to register the whole process.

Of course comfort eating is a huge problem for many of us. This is something that I've had to deal with a lot since giving up alcohol. They call it 'trying to eat away your emotions', I think it is a good description of the condition. It is a habit that we pick up in childhood when we learn to associate our favourite foods with reward; usually this is junk food like chocolate or fatty meals. When we are adults we continue to make the association between this food and feeling good. When our emotions are out of control we turn to comfort foods as a means to make ourselves feel better. In the long run all this really does is make us fat and even more miserable.

Near the end of my drinking days I didn't care too much for food; eating felt like an unpleasant necessity most of the time. After getting the first beer of the morning down my throat the next chore would be getting some nutrition inside my stomach. Sometimes I would hit a pleasant level of drunkenness when I'd get the munchies, but for a lot of the time food was just a hassle.

When I gave up alcohol food took on a whole new meaning for me. I could now appreciate it. I began looking forward to mealtimes. Living in Thailand meant that there was a lot of great stuff to choose from. Oa is a fantastic cook so this encouraged my culinary experimentation. It didn't take me long to start turning to food for solace when things in my life felt stressful. No real surprise then that I started to pile on the pounds.

I hoped to use mindful eating to bring my weight down and to maintain this afterwards. I decided to track my progress on my website paulgarrigan.com. I reasoned that committing to an online diary would keep me motivated. The changes I planned to make to my lifestyle were not going to be too drastic, but I still felt hopeful that they would work to permanently solve my weight problems. As I said, my goal was to bring my weight down below 75kg and keep it there. I'd first need to lose 9kg to reach my target weight.

One of the nice things about my mindful eating plan was that it wasn't going to involve too much sacrifice; this was to be no crash diet where I'd slash calories and spend hours in the gym. If I felt hungry I'd eat. I'd also permit myself to consume as much as was needed to leave me feeling satisfied. The only real change would be that I wouldn't eat unless I actually felt hungry, and I'd stop eating as soon as I felt full.

Despite only making such simple changes to my life the results were impressive. I lost over 2kg in the first week. I noticed that most of my urges to eat were not related to hunger. A lot of the time I was going to the fridge just to get away from the computer. I discovered if I got up from the desk and walked around it worked just as well. By checking my motivations before eating I was able to avoid consuming a few hundred calories a day – all with no real effort on my part.

By staying more mindful it also meant consuming fewer calories when I did eat. I stopped filling my gob when my body felt full rather than waiting until all the food was gone. The hardest challenge turned out to be concentrating on the food. I tend to take my evening meal in my office. It's a bad habit I've developed because my wife and son like to have their evening meal later than me; I'm too hungry to wait. I usually watch a video on the computer, and it has become my favourite part of the day. I do try to concentrate more on my food, but it is one habit that I find difficult to break. If I've been working hard all day it means that eating while watching a video sort of feels like an earned luxury.

The results of mindful eating were impressive; not just the weight loss itself, but the ease by which I'd done it. Within a month I'd lost 6 kilograms, and by nine weeks I'd managed to get my weight down to 74kg. All I needed to do was keep mindful, and I'd never have to worry about weight problems again. In theory it seemed straightforward and foolproof, but I knew from experience how easy it would be for me to slip back into mindless eating. I definitely felt cautiously optimistic though.

People began to make comments about my weight loss. Khru Jack seemed particularly impressed. Most likely this was due to his conviction that this weight loss could be fully attributed to my weekly session with him at the gym. He looked so proud of the results that I didn't want to burst his bubble with the main reason for my weight loss.

When Tim, the owner of Sitsongpeenong, remarked on my changing body shape I did tell him about mindful eating. I could see his eyes glazing over at my mention of using meditation to lose weight. I suspected that he viewed my claims as a tad weird. He gave me a few tips based on his idea of the proper way to lose weight. I sort of felt miffed at this because mindful eating already seemed to be the perfect fit for me. My policy tends to be that if something is not broken you shouldn't try to fix it – not that I always follow this policy in practice.

My weight came down and I felt a whole lot better about myself. I still had a bit of a spare tyre around my stomach, but this could be hidden with a t-shirt. I wasn't as self-conscious about my flabbiness anymore. I'd also be free to join my son on the activities at Funarium without worrying about being responsible for a disaster. I also noticed that losing the weight had greatly increased my energy levels. I would still be struggling by the fifth round of pads, but I recovered much faster. The 30 second break in-between rounds was suddenly enough for me to recharge.

Chapter 12

By the beginning of December my enthusiasm for Muay Thai had begun to wane. I'd been pleased with my initial progress but found it hard to keep the momentum going with only one class a week. I did train almost every day at home, but it became something I wanted to get out of the way before enjoying my evening meal. I'd had such high expectations for my return to martial arts, but it just wasn't turning out as I'd hoped. I could see what the problems were, but I just did not know how to fix them. I didn't want to give up on Muay Thai, but I needed more than what was currently on offer.

It just no longer felt like I was back doing martial arts – that was the real problem. It seemed more like a fitness class where I just happened to be doing kicks and punches. I would go every week to Sitsongpeenong and repeat the same process each time. I'd obviously given Khru Jack the impression that I just wanted him to focus on my fitness level. Very occasionally he would add a new technique, but mostly my training didn't seem to be going anywhere. I didn't feel like a Nak Muay at all.

I missed the grading system that came with the other martial arts I'd practiced; just some type of syllabus to follow would have been nice. Even the Tai Chi class I'd attended in London handed out belts. I know that grading in an art like Tai Chi is considered sacrilege by purists, but I liked having something to work towards. It let me know what I needed to focus on for my level. The promise of learning new techniques in the future also motivated me to keep going. It's the same reason I like to play video games – I want to get to the next level.

When learning Lau Gar Kung Fu the grading system definitely motivated me. I remember I had this flimsy white book which I cherished dearly. It was made from cheap paper, and it only consisted of a few pages stapled together, but this became one of my favourite books at the time. It contained the full Lau Gar syllabus. All the belts were listed along with the techniques I would have to learn to achieve that belt. It only took a couple of minutes to read the whole book, but I would spend hours going over the information. It excited me to think about all these techniques that I would learn in the future; they all had exotic sounding Chinese names next to the English explanations.

In the Muay Thai class there didn't seem to be any real plan. Khru Jack had taught me a few basic techniques, and we just hammered these out every week. I'd no real idea about my progress because we didn't seem to be on a path to anywhere. It just became my weekly workout. This wasn't what I'd envisioned when I took up the classes. I wanted to develop some skills and feel part of something bigger than a fitness class. I knew that the problem wasn't Khru Jack or Sitsongpeenong; a lot of my disillusionment boiled down to my unreasonable expectations for what could be achieved with one class per week.

The idea of grading in Muay Thai is a controversial subject. There are classes in the West where they use such a system, but it isn't common in Thailand. It could be justly argued that Muay Thai has survived perfectly well for hundreds of years without any grading system- it goes back to the argument that if something isn't broken you shouldn't try to fix it. The main objection to grading is that it would be a bit meaningless. Thai fighters will often have trained thousands of hours by the time they hit their teens. It would be difficult to rank such effort using a system of belts; the worth of a fighter is decided by fighting. I could just imagine the scene if a foreigner arrived in a Thailand Muay Thai class wearing a black belt – it wouldn't be pretty.

The real danger of a grading system in Muay Thai is that it would give some people a false sense of security. Those who are more advanced might feel so protective over their status that they live in fear of anyone of a lower grade showing them up. This isn't really a helpful attitude for a fighter – it has to be about testing your skills against other people. Even somebody who is new to the sport can prove to be a tough opponent in sparring. During a fight a less experienced fighter could land one good punch and put their opponent on the defensive. Not having a grading system is a reminder that everyone is equal when they get into the ring.

I understand the arguments against grading in Muay Thai, but it is harder for me to train without this type of incentive. It just would have been nice to have something to work towards. This isn't such a problem for the full-time student because they always have their next fight to keep their attention. This is the difference between Muay Thai, and a lot of the other martial arts; without belts the only thing to really work towards are future fights. Because of this modern Muay Thai can feel more like a sport than an art. It is probably why urban Thais are more likely to sign up for a foreign Tae Kwon Do class than their own home-grown martial art. Let's be honest here, the reason why so many popular martial arts now have belts is that they are great for business.

It now seemed obvious to me that the trainer wouldn't take me too seriously if I wasn't preparing for an actual fight. I was just somebody who turned up every week for a bit of a workout. As long as Khru Jack made me sweat a bit he'd done his job. The techniques for modern Muay Thai are to be used in the ring. I wasn't even sparring; so a lot of the subtlety of the techniques wouldn't mean much to me anyway. I suspected that a lot of the technical aspects of this martial art only made sense after you had experienced fighting.

The other thing that I sort of missed in the practice of Muay Thai was formal sets of movements. I know people criticize these forms as just a waste of time. It is true that they are probably not going to be much benefit when it comes to preparing for combat. However I think there is something so graceful and meditative about these movements; it is possible to completely lose yourself in an intricate form. Of course Tai Chi is all about the forms, and this is what attracted me to that particular martial art.

The nearest thing that Muay Thai has to the forms

would be shadow boxing. I've watched some experienced Nak Muay fighting the air and there is undoubtedly a great deal of grace in their movements. They may not be following any set pattern of techniques, but it is obvious that they are entirely absorbed in what they are doing. In their mind they are fighting an opponent so their movements are defensive as well as offensive. I love the way the skilled Nak Muay is able to smoothly flow from one technique to another when shadow boxing – they seem to do it so effortlessly. I've also seen Thais performing Muay Boran (traditional Muay Thai) and this involved a predetermined set of movements; it looked like a dance. Of course the ram muay and wai kru that the Nak Muay performs before a fight do involve set movements, but these are not related to actual fighting in the same way as a form.

Khru Jack always got me to shadow box before beginning the pad session. This allowed him to judge how my technique was coming along. He never said anything, but I knew that my performance didn't impress him – it didn't impress me either. I always felt clumsy and there would be pauses instead of a nice flowing movement. I found it hard to imagine an opponent as I'd no experience of being up against one. This meant that I'd just fire out random techniques; combinations that could never work in a real fight. My movements were about as far away as you can get from a graceful martial arts form. To the onlooker my attempt at shadow boxing probably looked similar to a malfunctioning robot.

One private class a week is nowhere near enough to develop in a martial art. I remember when my father took up Kung Fu he could only train for one day a week. My dad put a lot of heart into this one session, but he seemed to just bob along and progress came slow. My father wanted to train more but he just couldn't manage it because of work commitments. After a couple of years he lost interest; just like I was doing now after a few months.

I did try to renew my enthusiasm for Muay Thai by buying books, watching YouTube videos, and visiting websites devoted to this combat system. But this sort of made me feel worse as it only emphasised how much my skills were lacking. I also began to question my decision to do private classes. An important element of Nak Muay development involved spending time with other students; you learn so much from being with other people.

My expectations for Muay Thai were overambitious to begin with. I wanted to recapture the same level of intensity that I'd experienced in my teens, but it could never happen. I now had grown up responsibilities so such devotion would no longer be possible. I've also found out that as we grow older it affects the way we relate to things – a sort of dulling effect. I've noticed this with my love of music; it just isn't quite as emotionally charged as before.

I've always loved music. I continued to hold onto the dream of being a famous singer and guitarist well into my thirties. During my teens I tried to put a couple of bands together, but they never got further than the planning stage. My curse was that I'd no talent. People would lose interest in joining my band when they figured out my skill level; it usually only took a few chords. I would often complain bitterly that nobody else had so much passion for something they had so little talent for. I've been learning guitar on and off for about 28 years, but I still can't convincingly play one song all the way through. I'm far more suited to air guitar than the real thing.

Music continues to be an important part of my life but my passion for it has noticeably declined over the years. Songs once meant so much to me; they felt as important as food. The impact that a tune used to have on my mood could be dramatic. I could physically feel every note sometimes. This connection with music probably reached its peak during my mid-twenties; then it was the sounds of the Pixies, Blur, Billy Bragg, and Nick Drake that meant so much to me. My music sometimes took me to the edge of madness; during one suicidal period I listened to the Nirvana song 'Marigold' continuously for hours – the same tune over and over again. I don't miss the darker effect that music had on my mood, but I do miss how it could really lift my spirits. Music still gives me great joy, but it doesn't lift me up nearly as high as before.

Over the years I've had periods of obsession with most types of music; even classical music. The only style that I never could get a handle on was jazz; that is until I started writing for a living. I now listen to smooth jazz radio when I'm working. I find any other type of music is too distracting. I can't listen to any songs with words because I end up accidently adding the lyrics to whatever it is I'm writing. I know some writers listen to relaxation music. I've tried this but it seriously reduces my productivity; I become sluggish and tired. So music definitely still affects me but just not as much as it once did.

I expect that this same dulling of emotional impact with age must also apply to martial arts. Maybe I can never feel quite as passionate about anything like that again. It may have been that strange mix of racing hormones that makes things so special when we are younger. Of course this doesn't mean that I need to stop doing things just because they are not going to be quite as wonderful as they were before – that would be just ridiculous. I can see that there is still plenty of joy and interest to be found in something like martial arts so long as my expectations are not unreasonable.

I missed one Saturday class at Sitsongpeenong because I was ill. I skipped the next one because of pure laziness. I managed to drag myself to a couple more classes after that, but my heart was no longer in it. By mid-December I'd stopped going altogether. I felt bad about giving up on Muay Thai, but promised myself that I'd start again in the new year. I sent an email to Sitsongpeenong to let them know that I'd be taking a break from the private lessons. January and February came and went, and I still felt too busy to make the class. It started to look like my return to martial arts had been short-lived.

Chapter 13

My failure to find a way back into martial arts bugged me. I felt like a fraud. I'd written posts on my blog about how a life away from the booze meant that I was now able to achieve my dreams. I meant every word at the time, but my recent performance made my claim appear hollow. I'd banged on about how important martial arts were to me, but here I was giving up after just six months. I feared that by giving up on Muay Thai, I'd be setting a precedent going forward. For the first four and a half years away from alcohol it felt like I had the golden touch – success seemed to come easy to me. I worried that by giving up Muay Thai I would be signalling the end of this golden age. It felt a lot more significant than just giving up on a new hobby – it sort of felt like I was giving up on myself.

The thought of writing a book about Muay Thai had been floating around in my head for a few months. I liked the idea but it also scared the shit out of me. I knew in order to make a book like that interesting it would need to involve a lot more than just weekly attendance at a private lesson. The format of such a tale would need to be along the lines of getting ready to fight or at least training full-time. Even the thought of getting into the ring filled me with panic. So while I liked the concept I decided that this was a project that would be best left on hold for a couple of years.

I'd wanted to write a book about my experiences working as a teacher in Thailand. I pitched the idea to my publisher in Ireland. I waited a few weeks hoping that no news was good news, but one evening an email arrived with a polite 'no thank you'. This response hit me hard. Maybe the only interesting thing that I had to offer publishers was my tale of escaping addiction at a Thai temple. Perhaps I'd never get to write another book.

In a panic I put together a new proposal pitching my Muay Thai book idea. I gave it the title, *Middle Aged Ex-Drunk Wants to Fight Muay Thai*. I doubted that such a name would ever make it on the cover of a book, but I hoped it would be enough to interest the publisher. I felt enthusiastic about the proposal and this made the pitch easier to put together. I knew it had the makings of a good story. I just worried about my ability to pull it off.

I had to wait another couple of weeks before the publisher responded to my proposal. I would check my email inbox every few minutes during the workday. Every time I heard the ping to signify that 'you've got mail' I would have butterflies in my stomach. I worried about what would happen if the publisher said no to my book proposal, but that wasn't the worst of it. My biggest fear was that they would say yes. On a couple of occasions I actually put together an email to say that I wanted to withdraw the proposal. It just felt like I was punching way above my weight.

When the go-ahead to write the book finally came

I tried to act suitably delighted. I did feel excited and pleased, but this was counterbalanced by my fears. What had I gotten myself into? The idea of training hard didn't bother me in the slightest. That was something that I wanted to do anyway; this book would provide the perfect motivation. My fear was about the possibility of an actual fight. I just didn't believe that it would ever be possible for me to summon the courage to step into a ring and invite another person to try and beat the shit out of me.

There have been periods in my life when I've been on the fringes of violence. I worked in bars during my late teens and early twenties; at some of these establishments the clientele attended as much to fight as they did to drink. I saw a lot of violence but usually managed to keep a safe distance from it. I could be an obnoxious loudmouth when I had a belly full of beer. My persona as a pathetic drunk though, meant that people let me get away with a lot – "don't mind him, he's just a gobshite who can't handle his drink". People would take one look at me and see that I wasn't a threat. On rare occasions my irritating comments would push people too far, and they would strike out. I never had to be hit twice before going to the floor and rolling up in a ball – this would usually be enough to satisfy their sense of justice.

I managed to make it through school without suffering too many beatings. I lived in dread of the bullies but usually managed to avoid being hit. I learnt early on that my small size – and lack of a violent streak – meant that I would never be able to punch my way through school. I found that making the tough guys laugh could be a good way to stay off their radar when it came time to handing out the punishment. I'd act the class clown because being hit by a teacher didn't seem like such a big deal. The bullies never really liked me, but there were plenty of other people in school worth picking on. By making them laugh I managed to keep out of the danger zone, most of the time.

I never physically bullied other people in school, but I probably did a lot of damage with my words. This was all part of keeping on the good side of the hard-nuts by making them laugh. I'd no reservations about taking the piss out of those who were the victim of bullies; even when these people were meant to be my friends. I always felt bad about it but reasoned that it was better to have the attention on them than me. I said a lot of hurtful things in my attempts to save my own skin; it is something that I still feel bad about today.

On a few occasions I did side with the other oppressed students and got a bit of a kicking for my troubles. These moments of crazy bravery would come from nowhere. I'd just get this urge to make recklessly insulting comments about people who would make my life hell for it. I'd always deeply regret it as soon as the words were out of my mouth, but I sort of wish I'd done more of this – it would have been something to be proud of.

When I began doing martial arts at 13 it greatly improved my self-confidence. I watched the Bruce Lee movies and *Kung Fu* series and had complete faith that learning such a combat system would make me almost invincible in a fight. I had visions of standing up to the bullies and not only beating them, but looking great as I did it. I wouldn't use my powers in a purely selfish manner; I'd also help the oppressed everywhere. I guess that many people around the world felt the same way after seeing Bruce Lee in action. He represented the small guy standing up to the bullies. He promoted the dream that even timid souls could learn to stand up for themselves. I'm no longer convinced that such a possibility is feasible, but believing in it for awhile helped me a great deal.

I diligently practiced Kung Fu every day at home and attended classes as often as I could – usually four or five times a week. My father felt relieved to finally see me doing something physical. He worried that I spent too much time indoors reading and listening to music. He wasn't really a sports fan, but he wasn't a book lover either. My dedication to martial arts impressed him so much that he decided to take it up with me. This sharing of a passion brought us closer together. He always expressed interest in my hobbies, but now I could see that he meant it.

Martial arts came into my life at exactly the right time. I struggled with life a lot back then. I just never felt like I fitted in anywhere. My family moved house a lot during my formative years and it would be easy to attribute this to my feeling of alienation, but I can see now that the problem ran a lot deeper than this. I just felt uncomfortable in my own skin and needed a way to escape this – too sensitive and self-absorbed by far. Even at age 13 I could feel a pull towards alcohol. I'd even tried it a couple of times. The stolen cans of beer had made me sick, but I still felt fascinated by what it could do for other people. It seemed to turn even the dullest characters into lovable rogues. I wanted some of that special happy juice. Perhaps if I had not found martial arts at that time I would have found alcoholism a lot earlier.

The philosophies attached to the eastern martial arts interested me a great deal. Buddhism and Taoism made a lot of sense to me. I tend to question everything; it is like an itch I can't leave alone. This inability to just accept things meant that I had questioned my way out of the Catholic beliefs I'd grown up with. I can now see that this religion works perfectly well for many other people, but at that time I wanted certainty – something that really doesn't exist in such an uncertain world. I've always had spiritual yearnings so losing my Christian faith so young hit me hard; it left a huge hole in my life that needed to be filled.

I didn't want a new religion, but I found that martial arts provided a framework for dealing with the world. Along with Kung Fu came meditation; this turned out to be the perfect tool for spiritual development. I hoped that it would satisfy my yearning to connect with something beyond the material world. Learning Kung Fu was never about becoming a Buddhist or a Taoist, but these philosophies offered new ways of seeing things. I found that a noble purpose would be to master the body and mind; achieving such mastery would ensure that my life would have meaning.

It is this idea of mastering the body and mind that still appeals to me today. This is really what I'm looking for in Muay Thai. I've had periods in my life where I've meditated intensively and I have had impressive results, but I suspect that even greater results can be achieved when both physical and mental work is combined. I'm not sure if the goal of this path is to reach some type of enlightenment; maybe there is nothing at the end of this process. I've found though that the real joy in life is to be found in the journey and not in the destination. There doesn't always have to be a final goal for something to be worthwhile. The only real purpose of using a goal was to get me off my arse and into action.

SO THE SPIRITUAL ASPECT OF my early martial art practice to became hugely important to me. Of course I also wanted become Bruce Lee, but it was his persona as a spiritual warrior, as well as a top notch fighter, that appealed to me most. I also loved the TV series *Kung Fu*. This show had been around since the '70s but there were still repeats on Irish TV. I couldn't get enough of it. The story of a Shaolin monk who wandered around America beating people up – TV doesn't get much better than that!

After I'd trained at Kung Fu for a year I began entering competitions – just light no-contact or semi-contact events. This would be my chance to get an ego payout for all that hard work. I made it to the quarter finals a couple of times in local competitions, but mostly I underperformed. The worst thing was that I'd get beaten by people whom I knew put less effort into training than I did. I don't think that these individuals were particularly talented; they just were able to stay calmer under fire. I seemed to be missing a key ingredient in my Kung Fu arsenal, and I worried that this might not be something that I could learn.

Around this time I witnessed a few proper fights where people did get hurt. Not the usual thing at school where kids would just push each other. I'm talking about full-force blows where the combatants were literally trying to kill each other – most often drunken fights over girls. Such confrontations made me realise that aggression wasn't something that you could learn – not that I'd want to anyway. There are psychos out there who live to fight, and a timid person is not going to win against them even if they do learn martial arts. Aggressive people don't care about getting hit; they just want to cause as much damage to their opponent as possible. They hit people because they love it; this type of passion cannot be faked.

I knew that I could never stand up to these guys in a physical confrontation. I would have to be prepared to kill to have any type of chance in a fight against them; hitting them without the willingness to destroy them would just make the situation worse. I just don't have that type of aggression in me; I guess most people feel the same which is a good thing. I've heard many stories of black belts getting beaten to a pulp, and I can understand why. Learning the right moves isn't enough; you need a certain type of mentality to survive as a street fighter. Later I got to know some of these psycho types, and they scared the shit out of me. They didn't seem to have any sense of guilt about hurting another human. I'm not sure if they were actual psychopaths, but they seemed to tick all the boxes for this condition.

One of the things I liked about the novel *Trainspotting* by Irvine Welsh was that the characters were so believable. I've never taken heroin, but I've met plenty of people who act almost exactly like those fictional druggies. The most convincing character of all was Begbie. Robert Carlyle played him perfectly in the movie. This psychopath would explode violently at the slightest provocation; those around him lived in fear. He would attack complete strangers out of boredom or if things weren't going his way. I'd met a lot of people who have this kind of winning personality. This type of nutcase exists, and no martial art will defeat them unless the person using it is ready to kill.

In my late teens I worked in a bar in Oxford. There were two rough looking young guys who were regulars there; one of them had tattoos on his neck. They were complete hard cases from Leeds, but they were friendly enough. They both liked me for some reason; probably because they both had grandparents who were Irish. These two fellows would occasionally insist that I join them for a drink during my lunch break. They would be willing to pay so they never had to ask me twice. We used to hit this bar that had a lock-in during the afternoons; this was when the pubs in England still closed in the afternoons. From the outside it would look as if the bar was closed but once you get inside it would be jam packed.

I always wondered how these two guys managed to have money all the time. Even though I liked them they still intimidated me. They likely had the same effect on other people so I couldn't imagine they had too many job offers. I guessed they were getting a bit of money from social welfare, but surely not enough to get pissed every day the way they did. It was while we were sitting in a bar one afternoon during my lunch break that they confided in me how they made their living – what they told me came as a huge shock.

I wouldn't go so far as to say these two guys were hit men, but it was pretty close to that. They would beat people up for money. They lived in Oxford but tended to do a lot of their work in London. They were telling me all this as if it was the most normal thing in the world. I was on my third pint of Kronenberg at this stage, and I'd had a lot to drink at work behind the bar that morning, so I was feeling brave enough to question them further. I wanted to know if they would kill someone for money; without hesitation they answered in the affirmative. They reassured me they had never gone quite that far, but one of them looked a bit disappointed to admit this.

The thing that freaked me the most about these two nut-jobs was that I could tell how they genuinely enjoyed beating people up. From their point of view they were living the dream; earning money for doing a job they loved. They went around slapping people anyway so why not get paid for it? They probably felt the same way about hurting their victims as I do about writing. I would imagine that these days they probably even have internet forums for people like this; somewhere they can share their passion with likeminded psychopaths. I'd never realised before this that there were people so fucked up in the world. They were nice guys to talk to, and were always buying other customers in the bar drinks, yet they were willing to beat up strangers without the slightest hint of remorse.

There would not be enough booze in Oxford to give me the courage to keep drinking with these two ruffians. I worried that if I kept hanging around with them they would eventually turn on me. I avoided them like the plague after this; when they came into the bar I'd try to look busy and let someone else serve them. They stopped coming into the bar a few weeks later; apparently they were arrested for armed robbery – it was such a relief to not have to be around them anymore. I didn't even feel sorry for them. I've never met two individuals who were more suited to prison life; they would be in their element surrounded by all that violence.

I'm not saying that everyone who wants to fight in a full-contact sport is some type of aggressive deviant. I do believe that there is a scale going from extremely passive to extremely aggressive, and that good fighters will tend to be more on the aggressive side of this scale. I understand why people enjoy watching fights, but the idea of getting in the ring for fun just didn't make sense to me – or at least it didn't up until recently. One of my few accomplishments as a drunk is my almost violence-free record. There were only three serious fights during that 20 year period and none of these left lasting injuries. This is quite an accomplishment; especially when I consider my propensity for winding people up the wrong way.

I want to be a martial artist, but this does not mean I want to be a fighter. It has never been the aggressive side of things that held my interest. As I've already said, I'm attracted to the self-mastery of it all. I enjoy the kicking and the punching because of the movements, and not because my aim is to hurt anyone. I enjoy the sweat and the pain of hard training. I want to beat the person I was yesterday and not my opponent.

While writing this book I've been forced to spend

quite a bit of time figuring out what it is exactly about martial arts that attracts me so much. It has a lot to do with my past. For a few years in my teens I felt comfortable in my own skin most of the time. I lost so much of my self-esteem during the years of addiction. It is understandable that my mind yearns for something that once gave me a sense of control – Kung Fu provided that. It just feels right that I should try to get back all that became lost to me.

Another reason why martial arts remains important to me is the association with my dad. It had been something that made him proud; after that I did so much to disappoint him. We had once been so close, but for many years I carried a great deal of resentment because he'd broken up our family. My parents' separation had heralded the end of my martial arts practice, and I blamed him for that too. My fall into self-destruction began at that time, but I certainly wasn't blameless in the whole affair – it took me years to figure this out.

It is no coincidence that I started training Muay Thai within weeks of my father's death. It became a way of feeling close to him again. I'm not convinced that an afterlife exists, but I just wanted to make him proud. By returning back to martial arts I could show him that my life was back on track. It meant more than turning up at his funeral to say nice things about him. I hate funerals. Not because of death but because so much of it is about the mourners. Drunks love to hijack people's funerals – look at how sad I am, please buy me a drink.

Chapter 14

So I was going to write a book about Muay Thai. This meant no more pussyfooting around with one private class a week – forget that. I'd need to put in a lot more time and energy to take things up a level. At the very least I'd need to start attending a regular class with other Nak Muay. The perfect conclusion for the book would be for me to fight. I could then have a *Rocky* type ending in the final chapter. I wouldn't have to win the fight, but getting knocked out in two seconds would be a bit boring for the reader. This meant that I'd need to train full-time to be ready for combat. I told the publisher that the book would be ready by the end of the year so that really only gave me about six months to train and fight. It looked to me like an impossible task, but I'd already signed up for it. I felt excited by the idea of trying to make it work. I'd be facing some of my greatest fears, and there is usually a nice payback in life when I do this.

I fired off an email to Sitsongpeenong to warn them of my return. I hadn't been to a training session in almost two months. I wanted reassurance that it would be fine for me to join in the regular class. I also enquired about the possibility of a fight if I trained sufficiently hard for a few months. Tim answered that there would be absolutely no problem for me to join in the regular classes. It would also be theoretically possible for me to fight after a few months of hard training, but we would need to wait and see how I progressed. I decided to return to Sitsongpeenong the following day; I could not afford any delay.

The most surprising thing about my first regular class was its similarity to a private lesson. I turned up on a Saturday afternoon, and there were no other foreigners in attendance. I later found out that a lot of people take this session off so that they can enjoy the weekend. The only trainer there turned out to be Khru Jack so this meant more or less business as usual. He needed to take care of a few Thai fighters, but he still managed to give me a lot of attention.

I felt a bit sheepish going back to the gym after my long absence. Khru Jack did seem a bit cool towards me at the beginning. Perhaps he thought that I'd turned up five hours late for our private lesson. The news about my decision to join the regular class obviously hadn't made it to him. It also turned out that he had not been informed of the email where I explained that I would be taking a break from Muay Thai – he assumed that I'd just stopped turning up without any notice. From his point of view my actions could fall under the category of 'taking the piss' so a bit of coolness in response to my arrival back in his world could be considered deserved.

I warmed up as usual on the stationary bike before doing a bit of pad work. I struggled hard through the five rounds, but it wasn't anywhere near as difficult as that first time. I actually felt quite pleased that my fitness level wasn't too bad. I had been training a lot at home in recent weeks so this had a lot to do with it. I'd also managed to keep my weight down at 75kg during the break from Muay Thai so this helped a lot too.

The Thai students were doing their own thing so it didn't really feel like a group class at all. I'd been looking forward to training with other people so I sort of felt a bit of disappointment with this lack of other foreigners. The only real difference from the private class was that it lasted a bit longer. I spent most of this extra time doing rounds on the bags. I actually enjoyed this a lot because Jack was too busy with the Thai students to monitor my exertions. I left the gym on a high – it felt nice to be back.

I'd conducted a bit of research on the normal routine for preparing to fight Muay Thai in Thailand. Foreigners normally trained for three months full-time before going anywhere near the ring, and these were mostly people who already had a bit of Muay Thai experience before arriving. Full-time training involved two sessions a day with each session lasting about two hours. It would not be possible for me to take three months out of my life to prepare for a fight – I had too many commitments and not enough money. This meant that the project was already off to a bad start. I did not allow myself to become too despondent but instead focused on possible solutions.

The problem wasn't just taking four hours out of my day to train – I could probably just about manage that. It would be the travelling between the gym and home that would make it unworkable – that would suck up another four hours of my day. The only possible solution would be to do a lot of the training at home.

If I could workout for an hour or two in the mornings and then go to the gym in the afternoons then this could be a feasible solution. I could then arrange to go to Sitsongpeenong full-time in June for the build-up just before the fight. That way I'd only be losing out on a month of work rather than three months.

I sent another email to Tim at Sitsongpeenong; this time outlining my plan to train for a fight with half the training done at home and half at the gym. He got back to me saying that it could possibly work. It will all depend on my ability to do a lot of tough cardiovascular training under my own steam. I could understand his concern because there is the temptation to take things easy when there is no trainer around. In order to get ready for a fight I would need to push myself way beyond my comfort zone. I reassured Tim that this would not be a problem, but I wasn't fully convinced myself. I'd no experience of training at that level of intensity so had no way of knowing how I'd react.

It was now near the end of March and I hoped to fight by the end of June. I didn't have much time at all. I knew that if I took on too much right away that I'd end up getting injured so I made a plan to build up my workload on a weekly basis. I'd start off with two 40 minute sessions at home; one in the morning and one in the evening. On days when I would go to Sitsongpeenong I could skip the evening session at home. I'd start by attending two regular classes each week, and then add an additional class each week going forward after that. By the end of April I wanted to be training an hour each morning at home and attending the gym at least five times a week – an ambitious plan but probably achievable.

I later regretted becoming so fixated on fighting at the end of June. My reason for choosing that date boiled down to being overly eager – it was never realistic. I felt excited about the training and wanted to get stuck in right away. I reasoned that by aiming towards a date near in the future it would force me to buckle down. I always work better when I'm under pressure to meet a deadline. Once that date got locked in my brain it became intractable. Maybe if I'd been a bit more flexible with my timing things would have turned out differently.

I had one event on the horizon that would interfere with my fight preparations. My mother would be arriving in a couple of weeks to pay us a visit. She would be travelling a long distance for her first trip to Thailand – unless you class a previous two-hour stopover at Bangkok airport as a visit (which strangely enough she does). I couldn't just expect her to spend the time watching me get ready for a Muay Thai fight. She would be staying with us for a month, and I'd need to devote at least a couple of weeks of that to showing her around. I wanted to make sure she had a good time. If she got to see a few places I wouldn't feel so bad that she would be spending the rest of the time with my wife and her grandson.

Chapter 15

MY NEXT REGULAR MUAY THAI class did include a few
other foreigners, and this time there were plenty of
trainers around too. Khru Jack commandeered me as
soon as I came through the door. As usual he told me
to get going on the stationary bike. I saw everyone else
warming up with skipping ropes so I felt like a bit of
an old man on the bike. I had been practicing with
my rope at home, but couldn't get past five minutes
before giving up. These guys were still skipping after
20 minutes and by then I felt grateful to be slowly
pedalling along on the bike.

Khru Jack let me know that I'd be doing pads with
him again, but not until later. He needed to work
with one of the other foreigners first. The teacher told
me to get busy on the punch bag in the meantime. I
liked this plan because it would delay the hard work.
I also suspected that if he worked with somebody else
beforehand he would have less energy to push me hard.
I justified my lazy attitude with the idea that I needed
to ease into the tougher training regime gently in the
beginning. I also liked hitting the punch bags because
I could kid myself that my technique didn't suck – this
is easier to do when the target isn't moving. Before I
could go anywhere near the bag I would need to put
on my wraps.

In the private class the trainer had always put on the hand wraps for me. I knew that this was a bit of an indulgence, but it also made my life easier. I'd practiced putting the wraps on at home but made a mess of it every time. Joining the regular class meant accepting a less exclusive level of service so I set about putting on my own hand wraps. I sat down and tried to remember the way I'd seen the trainers do it in the past. I couldn't remember the exact pattern, but by the time I'd finished it looked satisfactory to my untrained eye. As soon as I moved my hands I saw that these pieces of cloth were a bit loose. I hurriedly stuck my hands into the gloves before all my hard work could fall apart.

I moved over towards one of the bags and began moving through my repertoire of Muay Thai techniques; all the time doing my best to look purposeful and experienced. I obviously didn't do a good job of it because one of the other students felt the need to come over and give me a few pointers. Darren was a friendly faced Australian who didn't try to sugar-coat the truth, that my technique sucked big time. He demonstrated a few kicks on the bag to show me how they should be done. I felt grateful for the advice but couldn't help feeling like the class dunce. It was OK for him; he looked like a natural fighter as he towered over me and flexed his muscles. I tried to make my moves closer to his, but it just made everything feel awkward. I obviously still had a lot to learn.

Darren left me to it. I continued to work on the revisions to my front kick that he had just demonstrated. He would look over occasionally and each time his face showed disapproval. I just wasn't getting it. In fact I found it impossible to follow the instructions he had just given me. I didn't doubt his knowledge and skill, but his way of doing things differed from Khru Jack and Khru Ton. Now my front kick lacked power and I looked stupid. I wanted to move onto something else but felt obliged to stay with this one technique because this guy had been good enough to try to do me a good turn. I couldn't help but lament that so many of my troubles these days began when other people tried to help me.

I didn't doubt that my Muay Thai technique sucked big time. The problem with private classes is that it had allowed me to develop a false sense of improvement. I had undoubtedly gotten somewhat better over those few months of private lessons but more so in my fitness level than in my technique – I had suspected this and now here came the confirmation. Over the next few weeks the problems with my techniques became even more glaringly obvious to me. It turns out that I was doing almost everything wrong; when it came to technique I found myself back at square one.

During the pad work with Khru Jack I suffered the consequences of my poorly assembled hand wraps. In between rounds I made the mistake of taking a glove off so that I could pick up a glass of water at the side of the ring. The hand wraps came loose and were now hanging half way down my arm. I tried to stuff it all back into the glove but this did not help. I kept on having to stop throughout the round to push bits of wrap back inside the glove. I felt like the whole gym was looking at me like I was an idiot. I should have just stopped and redone the wraps properly, but I have this stubborn streak that often stops me from doing the sensible thing.

Not only were the hand wraps not giving me any protection or support, but they were actually making things worse. At one point I punched the pad and I felt my wrist move in an odd angle – pain shot up my arm. I worried that I might have done some serious damage. I became reluctant to punch hard after that. Khru Jack kept on shouting at me to hit harder, but I just kept on tapping the pads weakly when it came time to punch. I could see that he was getting a bit pissed off so I tried to explain about the wraps and the pain. I think he believed me. He ended the session on the pads early. I felt relieved to be able to leave the ring and get my wraps sorted.

I fell into conversation with Darren. We were joined by a confident looking American guy called Peter. The two of them had only come to Thailand this time to train, but both of them had previous experience in the ring. I explained my plans to fight at the end of June, and they were good enough not to laugh right in my face. They said it might just be possible, but that I'd have to put in a huge amount of effort to be ready in such a short period of time. They had only just met me, but they could see that such an undertaking fell way beyond my current skill set. I knew they weren't trying to be nasty or anything – they were just telling me the truth as they saw it. My classmates both agreed that I should forget about fighting for the time being and just focus on training. I felt a bit gloomy as I left the gym; once again reminded of the enormity of the task that lay ahead of me.

Chapter 16

THE ASPECTS OF THE FIGHT preparations that I felt most optimistic about were my physical fitness level and mental readiness. These would both be within my control. Pure determination would be enough to get me into great physical shape; so long as I didn't get injured it shouldn't be too difficult. The real problem would be improving my technique and learning how to cope with being hit – bearing in mind that this other person would be trying to hurt me. Even if I did manage to build up my skills to an impressive level there was no way that I'd be able to escape being hit by my opponent. My natural reaction of rolling up into a ball would not be effective in a Muay Thai match. I'd read that staying mentally calm took much of the sting out of being hit. I hoped that my years of meditation would help with this; that it would give me a much needed edge when it came to mental readiness for a fight.

One of the parts of the body that takes a lot of abuse in Muay Thai is the shin. Not only do you use it when kicking, but it is also needed for defensive purposes. The turning kick is the most effective and therefore most frequently used of all strikes; it often involves slamming into the opponent with the shin. A common way to defend against this strike is for the defender to raise their own shin above the waist so as to protect the body. This means that in a Muay Thai fight there can be a lot of shin on shin contact. A hard strike to this part of the body is painful and leaves a bruise afterwards. During a Muay Thai fight the shin may need to absorb hundreds of direct hits.

I decided that one of the things I could do myself as part of the fight preparations would be to toughen up my shins. I'd watched all the movies and knew that the traditional way for Muay Thai fighters to do this would be for them to kick the trunk of banana trees. They would do this regularly so that almost all the feeling in that part of the body would be gone, they destroyed the nerves. I'd read that Thai fighters would end up suffering for this abuse in later life, but at least they had tough enough shins to last the pace of a fight.

I didn't fancy the idea of kicking the trunk of a banana tree – at least not to start with anyway. We actually have a banana tree in our garden, but the house is rented and the owner might object if I begin destroying the vegetation. I guessed that there must be a more modern approach to shin-toughening so I did an internet search to find out my options. I came across a suggestion that at first seemed a bit bizarre, but definitely sounded more appealing than kicking a tree. It involved using a rolled up wet towel to whack the shins for conditioning. I went on YouTube and found a few videos of people using this conditioning technique.

Oa volunteered one of my son's old towels for my shin conditioning regime, but that just didn't feel right. I can get a bit sentimental sometimes about silly things.

I worried that perhaps my wife and I will one day treasure these pieces of cloth – especially when Timmy hits adulthood and has no real time for us anymore. Maybe these towels from his infancy will then feel like precious gems to us. I knew that we had a whole bag full of them, but it still didn't feel right. I opted instead to sacrifice an old t-shirt. I'd had it in my wardrobe for over a decade, and still wore it regularly. Oa complained that I needed to stop wearing clothes that were falling apart. This t-shirt had come from the time when I still cared about looking smart; it was one of the last remnants left from that period. It now appeared closer to a rag than a garment somebody should wear. At least by using it to toughen up my shins I would extend its useful lifetime a bit longer.

Before arriving in Thailand I could be very fussy about my wardrobe. Even during those years of being a complete piss head I'd try to ensure that at least some of my money went on nice clothes. I would never have been described as trendy looking, but I did put a bit of effort into my smart-casual appearance. I suffered from snobbishness about labels and would look down my nose at cheap clothing. However, something happened after moving to Thailand. I changed from being a label snob to a fashion slob. I think it has a lot to do with the heat and how it limits wardrobe choices. These days most of my clothing comes from the Thai version of Tesco, and I tend to wear these items until they fall apart. If you'd told me before I came to Thailand that I'd be wearing clothes from a supermarket I would have been a bit horrified. These days I couldn't care less. I suppose getting married and giving up on pubs also has something to do with my loss of interest in clothing. I'm no longer trying to compensate for anything – well not as much anyway.

I borrowed one of my wife's plastic cooking bowls and filled that with water. I don't mean to sound sexist here by calling it her bowl as if anything to do with the kitchen is her domain. When I say it was 'my wife's' I literally mean that it is something she bought even before I met her. Anyway I digress. I had watched a video on YouTube and saw how the guy had soaked his towel in water before rolling it up tightly to expel most of the fluid. He would then strike his shin with the rolled up damp towel.

When I rolled up the t-shirt it didn't look anywhere near as tight and effective as the shin-blaster made by the guy in the video. One of the problems with my design was that the t-shirt's arms were still hanging down loosely. I tried to tuck them into the folds of the rolls, but they kept on slipping back out again. The t-shirt was made from thin material so this also made it less effective than a towel. I decided to forge ahead anyway. I tentatively gave my shin a wallop, and it didn't feel too bad. Oa and Timmy had come outside to observe my latest crackpot plan. I'd tried to explain the reason behind the madness to Oa but she just didn't get it. She also refused to accept that a Thai person would be crazy enough to kick banana trees even after I supplied her with photographic proof of this.

The guy in the YouTube video had recommended hitting each shin fifty times so that is what I did. After every few slaps I'd put the t-shirt back into the water and roll it up again. The strikes weren't painful, but the t-shirt sleeves would sometimes sting the side of my leg when they landed. The muscles in my arms felt a bit sore, but giving that part of my body a workout would be an added bonus. I finished both legs and to be honest I didn't notice much of a difference. Maybe I really did need to use an actual towel to get the benefits.

Over the next few days I repeated this process with the wet t-shirt. Near the end of the week bruises started to form on each shin. These were quite painful to the touch, and my next session on the pads at Sitsongpeenong turned out to be agony because of it. My right shin felt the worst, and I had to tell Khru Jack that I wouldn't be able to use that leg anymore that day. It meant using my left all the time; this wasn't such a bad thing because my weaker leg would benefit from the extra attention. It added a new element of challenge to the pad session, but at least my sore right shin would get a chance to recover.

Near the end of the class I told Tim about my experience with the wet t-shirt. He looked at me as if I'd completely lost the plot. He didn't think that there was any need for such extremes and warned that I could be doing a lot of damage to myself. He reassured me that just working on the pads and the bags all the time would be enough to condition my shins. So in the end my t-shirt ended up in the bin anyway. My new hobby of self-flagellating with a wet t-shirt ended there thankfully.

My next idea to help prepare for the fight turned out to be a bit more successful. A recurrent concern of mine had been the amount of time I sat at the computer. I assumed that working as a writer meant that there would be no way around this. I would spend up to 12 hours a day sitting on my arse, and it was doing my health no favours. I worried that even with twice-a-day training I would undo a lot of this good work by sitting around the rest of the time.

The idea of a stand up desk appealed to me, but it sounded a bit whacky. I'd found a few videos where people were using this type of desk; in one of these clips the guy had a treadmill and walked as he typed away on his keyboard. It looked wonderful, but I wondered how it would impact productivity. Would it really be possible to walk and still type all day on a keyboard? The best plan would be to start with a basic stand up desk before moving on to anything too fancy.

The more I investigated the stand up desk the more it sounded like the perfect answer for my health concerns. It would be such a relief to find a solution to this negative aspect of my work. I did a search online to find out the cost of a stand up desk; even the most basic model had a jaw-dropping price tag. There would also be the problem of getting such an item in Thailand. I'd never seen them on sale, and I'd no idea where to look. I felt crushed. Then the obvious solution hit me; I'd make my own.

I'm really bad when it comes to DIY projects. I'm just too clumsy with that type of thing. I've no patience for it. I hate buying furniture that comes in flat packs because I make a mess of even the simplest assembly. I always end up with something that doesn't look right and soon falls apart. I've wasted a lot of money on this type of furniture. Oa on the other hand has a real knack for this kind of work. She made me a desk from bits of wood, and she is always making bookshelves for our home – my switch to the e-book reader is frustrating this passion of hers now though. I knew that she would enjoy the challenge of a stand up desk.

I did a bit more research online and found out that making a stand up desk could be incredibly easy. It only took a few adjustments to a normal desk; it could be created using bits of junk from around the house, so I went scavenging. I found a small table in our spare room. I put this on top of my desk and moved the computer monitor onto it – this raised the screen to almost eye level. I then used some plastic storage containers to build a platform for my keyboard. I'd only meant this to be a temporary solution until my wife got to work on the proper desk, but it turned out to be so successful that I've kept it. It doesn't look very fancy, but it gets the job done.

Using the stand up desk did feel a bit strange initially. I could still type perfectly well, but it just felt a bit awkward – no worse than working with a new keyboard, but it did slow me down initially. By the end of the first day I felt completely knackered from all that standing. The second day turned out to be easier. By the end of the week I hardly even noticed that I was using a stand up desk.

The benefits of my new furniture more than made up for any initial discomfort. I would be more tired at the end of the day, but I had more energy throughout the day. I no longer felt tied to the desk, and when the mood hit me I could just lash out a few Muay Thai kicks to loosen up my body. If my mind became stuck while writing I could just take a few steps away from the screen and stare out the window. This turned out to be more beneficial than just staring at the monitor and fuming.

I knew that realistically the stand up desk was unlikely to make that much difference to my fight preparations. Mentally it did give me a boost to know that I was now living a healthier life. I did seem to have a bit more energy in the next few training sessions but maybe that could have been purely psychological. Even Oa had to admit that this had been one of my better crazy ideas.

I could feel myself falling into the pace of the fight preparations by the time my mother arrived in Thailand. It felt great to have her over for a visit – my son loved the extra attention. I also welcomed the chance to get away from work for a few days. I had not had a real break since beginning work as a freelance writer almost two years previously. We took a trip down to the Eastern seaboard – we had a few days in Rayong before moving on to Pattaya. The weather turned out to be uncharacteristically cloudy for the time of year, but personally I welcomed the break from the unbearably high temperatures that usually come with the cloudless April sky.

I'd only intended to interrupt training for a week during my mother's visit, but on the last day of our trip I ate a dodgy four-cheese pizza. I ended up staying in bed for a week and only got out of it to go to the toilet to vomit. I'm not good at being sick – or maybe I'm too good at it. During my years working as a nurse I noticed how some patients were inspirational and stoic when faced with illness. Their body would be doing all sorts of unpleasant things but they wouldn't complain. They just did their best to get on with life. When I get sick I just want to roll up into a ball and hide. I can work through a cold, but anything stronger than that and I'm off to bed – all my attention is then focused on feeling sorry for myself.

Chapter 17

I'D NOW BEEN TRAINING AT Muay Thai for almost eight months (with a two month break along the way), and I'd still not experienced any type of sparring. This obviously worried me because I planned to fight in a couple of months. I'd heard that normally a Nak Muay would have hundreds of hours of sparring practice under their belt before going anywhere near a proper fight. This was a part of training that I'd been dreading from the start, but I needed to begin getting proper fighting experience right away; otherwise there would be no chance of me being ready in time. My previous experience with Kung Fu sparring wouldn't be of much value to me now as that had involved hardly any contact. In Muay Thai fighters were discouraged from trying for knockouts while sparring but people did still get hurt – mostly the foreign fighters as they tended to get a bit carried away.

Before learning to spar with punches and kicks I first had to learn how to clinch. This is called plam Muay in the Thai language. It involves using hands, shoulders, body weight, and knees to control the opponent. In Western boxing when the fighters clinch they will be separated; they are just using it as an opportunity to rest. In Muay Thai a lot of the action will occur in the clinch as fighters can fire out devastating knees and elbows from this position. It is therefore vital that anyone who wants to last in a Muay Thai fight knows how to handle the clinch. I noticed at Sitsongpeenong that they only rarely bothered with regular sparring, but fighters would do clinching at almost every session. The Thai fighters seemed to spend hours just doing plam Muay.

My introduction into clinching came without warning. I'd just finished on the pads and now looked forward to taking it easy on the punch bag but Khru Jack called me back into the ring. I say call, but he did not actually use words. Instead he did this strange movement with his shoulders; he looked like somebody running for the bus in slow motion – it turned out to be his sign language for clinching. I'd no idea what he meant and hoped that he might be signalling somebody else. I even looked behind me to make sure. His now slightly irritated "yes, you" left me in no doubt about whom he was referring to. He climbed back outside of the ring to help me remove my gloves and hand wraps. Clinching is a lot easier when your hands are free.

I'd noticed other people clinching, but I'd no real idea of what it involved. I expected Khru Jack to explain the rules but instead he just matched me up against this other Westerner. I stood awkwardly in front of my opponent feeling like a complete moron; just waiting for somebody to tell me what I was meant to be doing. The other guy looked to be a lot heavier than me and a good foot taller. He'd only arrived at Sitsongpeenong and we had not yet been introduced. I didn't know if now would be a good time to introduce myself. I decided to keep quiet so as to avoid the babble that normally comes out of my mouth when I'm nervous. I didn't want this guy to know just how much of an amateur he was up against; maybe if I looked tough it would give me some type of advantage.

My opponent got the proceedings underway by firing knees at my stomach; luckily these were only taps. I noticed that everybody else seemed to have their arms wrapped around their opponent's neck so I did the same. I then basically just tried to hang on to him for the next few minutes as he moved from firing knees into my stomach to aiming them at my rib area. Every time I attempted to return a knee he would knock me off balance; many times I ended up on the mat. He threw me around like a rag doll, and I had no idea how to respond. I could feel my face burning with embarrassment for my ineptness.

Because my opponent towered over me he could easily push down my shoulders so that my face ended up completely exposed to his knees. My arms would be trapped, and I would be in no position to defend myself. He put me in this position repeatedly. If he wanted to he could have just comfortably kneed me in the face until he got bored; there would have been nothing I could do about it except plead for mercy. It was the most vulnerable position I could end up in during a fight, and this guy could put me there at will. In a real Muay Thai encounter it would have been game over.

Near the end of the clinching session my lack of skill got noticed by one of the trainers. He came over and suggested a couple of techniques I could try on my partner. He also explained that I had to keep my arms inside the opponent's arms; that way I'd have the most control. It turns out that much of the work of clinching involves trying to get your arms into this favourable position. I appreciated the advice, but I felt a bit too traumatised by my first clinching session to really listen and make use of it.

It came as a great relief when we were told to leave the ring and do some weights. I felt a bit surprised to find that despite being thrown around the place so much I had sustained no physical injuries; mentally though I felt like I'd just been through a war. I wasn't expecting a great performance with my first attempt at Plam Muay, but I'd hoped to at least have put in a noble beginner's effort – that certainly wasn't it.

I felt bad about my performance but it also motivated me. I made a promise to myself in the car on the way home – I would never let another person completely dominate me like that again. I would not be able to avoid facing people with better skills, but I could put up more of a fight next time. I wouldn't mind losing so much if I'd done my best. Of course the real problem this time had been my lack of knowledge about clinching. Was the idea just to control the opponent and fire in as many knees as possible? Or should I focus on trying to knock the other person off balance? I had no idea.

As usual I turned to the internet for answers. I'd no problem finding YouTube videos on the subject of Plam Muay. These did offer a few suggestions for what I should be doing. I found one technique in particular that appeared quite effective. It involved twisting the opponent as he went to knee me by tugging at his shoulder. He would already be a bit off balance so using this against him seemed like a perfect defence. There were other videos that suggested how I could prevent myself from falling into that danger zone where my opponent could knee me to death in the head. It involved lifting my hands over his arms and pushing at his chin every time he started to push me down. The defence made perfect sense now that I saw it.

At the next session at Sitsongpeenong I came with a head full of ideas for how to clinch. This time I showed no hesitation when Khru Jack made the funny gesture to indicate time for clinching. I climbed into the ring to face another new face; he looked to be more my size so I didn't feel so intimidated. I could tell from the start that his skills were high, but he didn't seem out to prove anything. He had no trouble dominating me, but for the most part he just took things easy. This gave me the confidence to experiment a little.

I tried my new clinching techniques, but it turned out that these were a lot harder in practice. I had no problem believing in their effectiveness, but I could see that timing was everything. My opponent would have already managed to strike with the knee before I got around to my attempt at pulling him off balance. Still, I had something to do, and this kept my mind busy. I didn't feel this time that my only job was to be just thrown around. As an added bonus I did manage to get a couple of knees in my opponent without falling on my arse.

In reality my performance that second time at clinching wasn't a great improvement on my first attempt. What did change was that I felt a tiny bit more in control. At least I had been attempting to attack and not just standing there while the opponent had his way with me. At the end of the clinching session I felt a tiny bit of jubilation. I doubt there would be many people who would have been so satisfied with such a dismal performance. I just felt like it proved how it would be possible for me to get better. I certainly couldn't be described as a 'natural' at clinching, but maybe one day I could climb to the heady heights of average.

Over the next few sessions there were further opportunities to practice clinching. Sometimes one of the trainers would pull my opponent off me to offer advice but most of the time they just left us to it. To be honest, I couldn't really notice any great improvement in my technique. Clinching just became something that I had to get through at the end of the session – something to get out of the way before I went home. We now had more foreigners at the gym and the usual routine was to divide the clinching into rounds with a new partner each round. At other times I'd just be put with one guy and we would be told to continue clinching until the trainer told us to stop; this could last anywhere up to 20 minutes.

I preferred sticking with the one guy for the full clinching session. No matter how good he was I could usually rely on him losing steam after a few minutes. Then it would just be a case of hanging on to each other and firing out the odd knee to keep the trainers happy. Changing partners every few minutes seemed to keep people energised. With multiple partners there would always be one who would be particularly vicious.

I sustained my first injury when clinching with a young French guy. It started out as a satisfying bout because we were both so evenly matched; neither of us knew what we were doing. The fun ended near the end of the encounter when he bit my eyebrow – he managed to remove a small chunk of flesh. This bite came as a result of an accidental clash between my forehead and his two front teeth. He seemed more concerned over my wound, but his mouth had taken a good wallop. Luckily neither of us suffered too much damage. I sort of felt a bit proud of my first Muay Thai wound.

Chapter 18

ONE SATURDAY AFTERNOON KHRU JACK paired me up with one of the young Thai fighters for Plam Muay. My opponent only looked to be about fourteen. There were no other foreigners in Sitsongpeenong that day so it was either clinch with the kids or nothing – I would have been happy with nothing. Instead I got to enjoy the surreal experience of being kneed and thrown around the ring by a kid one third of my size. I couldn't get near him. I've never tried to handle a slippery eel, but I imagine it's a similar experience. Luckily he was holding back on the power of the strikes because otherwise he would have demolished me.

I'd worked for almost seven years teaching in Thai schools. Many of the students were the same age as my opponent. It just felt wrong to be in the ring with someone like that. Even if I had the ability to put up a better fight I wouldn't have been willing to. I'd have felt like a bully and would have been too worried that one of my strikes would cause damage. I could see no benefit in this encounter other than to make me look stupid.

Some of the other young students had gathered around the ring and they were laughing at the performance. It must have looked like something out of a comedy movie where the giant gets beaten up by a dwarf. I knew that this young kid was more highly skilled than me, and had already been training full-time at Muay Thai for a few years, but it still hurt my pride. I felt angry with the teacher for putting me in this position. To be fair it wasn't really Khru Jack's fault. At the start of the lesson that day I'd stupidly made a comment about how I wanted more experience with Plam Muay but this definitely wasn't what I had in mind when I said it.

I hold conflicting opinions on the subject of kids fighting Muay Thai. My gut reaction is that it is a bad idea. These youngsters could get hurt and childhood is about enjoying life without having too many responsibilities. I do definitely believe that martial arts training can be very beneficial for kids, but fighting is another matter. One of the reasons why we decided on my son's school was that I liked the fact that they taught Tae Kwon Do as part of their curriculum. He is only barely out of nappies, but I still feel that it will benefit him by teaching discipline. It will also keep him active. There is no way that I'd allow him to fight Muay Thai though – not until he was in his very late teens at least. Even then, I'm not sure if I'd ever feel comfortable with him getting into the ring. I suppose that makes me a bit of a hypocrite; it is okay for me to do but not for him.

I try to not rush into harshly judging those aspects of Thai culture that bother me. This is because I know that life isn't black and white. I'm biased to view things in a certain way because of my own cultural heritage. I assume that children should live a certain way because that is what I've been brought up believing. If I heard that somebody in Ireland allowed young kids to fight full-contact martial arts I'd certainly feel a bit appalled by it.

In Thai culture people have traditionally been involved in Muay Thai from a young age. In poor areas kids will dream of becoming fighters in much the same way that children in other parts of the world will dream of becoming football stars. They know that Muay Thai can be a path out of poverty and a way to escape the predictability of rural life. Their heroes are the top fighters and it is only natural that they should want to be like them.

I worked in a Thai village school for five years and I saw firsthand how the opportunities for rural kids can be limited. The students are as intelligent and capable as children anywhere else, but they do not get the same opportunities. The teachers tend to assume that these children will grow up to be farmers and so the focus is just providing them with a basic education. Even if these kids manage to do well in school it can be a real financial hardship to go on to further education – so most of them will never get near the opportunity. By learning to fight Muay Thai they can take the future in their own hands. It is a career and at the very least it will allow them to experience something different than life in a village.

I see the youngsters that train at Sitsongpeenong and I do sometimes wonder if they have missed out on normal childhood things. Their life revolves around Muay Thai and they need to push their body to extremes. I also accept that this is what they have to do if they want to become the best. The reality is that no ambitious athlete can get to the top without sacrificing much of their teenage years. Muay Thai is not any different in this. Tiger Woods spent much of his childhood playing golf, but that is just the price he paid for greatness – other people dream of being in his shoes. The same is true for Muay Thai. It is not possible to become successful without making sacrifices, and these sacrifices may need to be made at an early age. If all the athletes agreed that nobody would start training until they were in early adulthood things would be different, but this is highly unlikely to ever happen.

MY REAL WORRY ISN'T ABOUT kids learning Muay Thai but with them stepping into the ring to fight. I could be overly concerned about this; the reality may be that fighting is no more dangerous than any other sport. It certainly can't be any more dangerous than kids riding motorbikes in Thailand; something that most teenagers do here. The youngsters involved in Muay Thai train hard and know how to protect themselves in a fight. They are professional athletes and most of their fights are won on points rather than knockouts. So I can understand the argument provided by those who defend kids fighting Muay Thai.

I do object to adults who view children merely as meal tickets; those who push the child too hard and don't do enough to ensure safety. I also worry that there are some kids out there who feel pressurised into fighting. I heard one of the other Western Nak Muay talk about how he witnessed a Thai father beat his young son because the boy had lost a fight. This is appalling and indefensible behaviour – no cultural differences can justify that. Unfortunately I suspect it is not an isolated incident. Of course Thailand is not the only country where some parents exploit their own children in search of fame and riches – it probably happens a lot less here than in some other places.

I have to admit that all the young fighters at Sitsongpeenong seem happy and well adjusted. They are top athletes just doing what they do best. Their life is Muay Thai and they seem well suited to it; I envy them their confidence. They are lucky enough to be training at one of the top gyms in Thailand. They already know that they are the cream of the crop. No matter what happens they will have something to be proud of for the rest of their lives. If I had the same opportunities at their age I wouldn't feel like I was missing out on anything. It is the type of childhood that other youngsters can only dream about.

I'm always impressed by those people who were able to get their shit together at an early age. Of course it makes me wonder what would've happened if I'd managed to do the same. Nowadays you hear about these kids who start successful businesses before they have even left school. It isn't like these individuals always come from privileged backgrounds or anything. They just seem driven to greatness at a young age.

It took me so long to figure out what I wanted to do with my life. My attitude in early adulthood was that so long as I get my shit together by the time I reached 30 it would be perfectly fine to not take life too seriously. I don't know where I got this idea from, but it certainly stuck with me; it became a blueprint for my life. It motivated me to begin my nursing training at age 27 so that I could be qualified at 30. I still had six more years of alcoholism after that, but in many respects my plan worked remarkably well.

I DON'T REALLY MIND BEING a late bloomer – it is certainly better than never blooming at all. I know that it is still possible for me to accomplish a lot even if I have been a bit slow out the gate. I actually feel like I've already found a lot of success in life. My financial situation isn't that great, but I have a lovely family, I live in a beautiful part of the world, and I have the job I dreamed about as a child. If this is as good as my life gets I wouldn't have much to complain about. There is this inner drive to always want more, but in so many ways my life is perfect right now – I just need to recognise this more.

I suppose another worry with the young Thai fighters is what is going to happen to them later on – after they hit their late twenties. They only have a few years to make a lot of money and unless they are exceptionally good they are not going to get the big purses. Even the champions struggle to make enough money to last for the rest of their lives. Once they have finished fighting the only real option for them in Muay Thai will be working as an instructor. But of course not everyone can teach or wants to teach. Maybe it is harder to have success early, and then spend the rest of your life without it, than to find success later in life. It must be hard to make it to the end of a Muay Thai career and have to figure out what you do next – maybe everything afterwards feels like an anticlimax.

When I first arrived in Thailand I stayed on the island of Koh Samui. I spent most of this time drinking in the same bar. To call it a 'bar' would be to exaggerate a bit; it was more like a straw hut that sold alcohol. It was perfect in location, but it was just something thrown together. The owner of this establishment was a guy in his thirties called Job. He had once been a successful Muay Thai fighter but the money from this was long gone. He now had to hustle hard just to stay afloat and this bar was part of that.

In reality the bar wasn't even Job's. His wife had put up the money for it. She financed it with cash sent to her by a Swiss boyfriend. When her foreign lover came to visit she would pretend that Job was her brother; they would all even share a house together like one big happy family. I did not envy Job the experience of lying in bed at night listening to his wife being bonked by a foreigner. I did like Job, but it all seemed a bit underhand and dishonourable. I'd seen the pictures of him as a successful Thai fighter but now here he was depending on the charity of a naive foreigner; pimping his wife to a Swiss guy just to make a few baht – how the mighty fall.

Job's bar never seemed to make much money. I stayed on Samui for about three months that time and became his best customer. From what I saw, Job always drank away any profit he made. He would be too intoxicated to manage the business properly; he gave too many free drinks away. At one time he must have been a highly disciplined person; how else could he have made a success of Muay Thai? Now he was just another piss head like me.

Chapter 19

I HAD NO REAL DIFFICULTIES keeping my weight around the 75kg mark. I still had a bit of a belly, but it was nowhere near as noticeable as before. I liked having a bit of fat on my cheekbones because people said it suited me. I hoped that my weight would fall a bit more as I moved into full-time training, but I wasn't particularly worried about it. I felt more concerned about building a bit of muscle to replace this last bit of fat.

Tim at Sitsongpeenong had arranged for a sports nutrition expert to come and give a talk at the camp. I gave a non-committed 'maybe' to the suggestion that I should attend. I felt proud of my achievements with mindful eating, and didn't really believe that any expert help would be needed. I'd learnt quite a bit about nutrition as part of my nursing training and arrogantly assumed that this was all that I needed to know. I also didn't believe that this guy would be able to tell me anything that wouldn't be found during a quick search on Google.

The internet makes it easy for 'know-it-all' people like me to cut out the experts, and this is not always such a good thing. It is particularly dangerous when it comes to health, because there is just so much crap written online. A lot of this advice can get people into serious trouble. During my years as a nurse I met quite a few individuals who had picked up nonsense ideas about their health based on things they found on the web. Near the end of my alcoholism I had no problem finding websites that promised to teach me how to drink like a gentleman – what a waste of time that turned out to be. I know the dangers of the internet too well when it comes to health problems but still it is the first and often only resource I turn to.

The main problem with health information on the web is that most of us will go hunting for things that confirm what we want to believe. I had found a lump in my testicles a few months before this. I spent days looking for information that would support my desperate hope that I didn't have testicular cancer. Eventually sanity prevailed and I did get the lump checked out by a professional. Luckily it turned out to be something minor, but it easily could have been the other way. If it had been serious I would have already wasted a lot of time before seeking treatment. So the internet can definitely be a dangerous tool in the wrong hands.

The nutrition expert came to Sitsongpeenong one afternoon when I wasn't training. Two of the guys at the gym who had been to the seminar gave enthusiastic endorsements for the event. According to them it had been a life changing experience. It sounded like they had been to a fanatical religious cult meeting rather than a nutrition lesson. They kept saying that it was a real shame that I hadn't been there and how it would have been so helpful to me. I began to feel a bit resentful about this. It was like these guys were saying that I was still a fatty in need of desperate help.

It was now getting near to my move to full-time training, and I wanted to have a clearer idea about who I'd be fighting at the end of June. I'd already mentioned this a few times to Tim. On each occasion he had given a confident reply. There would be no real problem finding me a suitable fight. This time when I asked him he appeared far less positive about the possibility. In fact as things stood he felt that it was going to be highly unlikely that I'd be ready in time.

Tim's main concern was my weight. At the moment I would be categorised as a super middleweight. The problem would be that the guys I'd be fighting in this class would be a lot bigger than me. They would be lean with a lot of muscle while I was a small guy who was carrying way too much excess fat. Tim laid it all out in simple terms; either I moved down to the welterweight category or I would be destroyed in the ring. In order to make that weight I would need to drop 8kg in a little over a month. Now I understood why people in the gym had been making such a big deal about my weight. I hadn't even considered how the weight categories in Muay Thai worked. I just assumed the fight promoter would pick somebody roughly my size. I'd been naive and now it would cost me.

I told Tim that I felt confident about losing the weight, but he wasn't convinced. Losing 2kg a week is easy when you have a lot to lose, but it would be harder for me to achieve this now that I'd already brought my weight down to a reasonable level. The real problem is that I'd need to lose the weight without losing too much muscle. Otherwise I'd still be out of my depth in the ring without enough power to do damage to my opponent. The more I thought about it the more I had to agree with Tim's pessimistic assessment.

Tim did provide me with one possible solution to my weight problems. He promised that if I could get my weight down to 70kg the week before the fight then we would be able to sweat the final 3kg off right before the weigh-in. I'd seen the other guys running around in a plastic sweat suit in the days before a fight and could see that it must be torturous in the Thai heat. Still, I would be willing to do it if it meant the difference between fighting and not fighting. Losing 5kg seemed achievable in a month and maybe I'd even manage more than this so that I could avoid the sweat suit.

Despite my claims Tim did not believe that I would be able to lose the weight without help. He wanted me to go see his sports nutrition friend so that I could be given a proper diet plan. He felt my vegetarianism complicated things even further; I'd need expert advice for reducing my calorie intake while not losing a lot of muscle. I still felt that I could probably achieve the goal myself, but kept this argument to myself. I worried that Tim would just rule the fight completely out of the question unless I saw this guy. I felt that at least by agreeing I would prove that I was taking the fight seriously.

The nutrition guy was called Brad. I telephoned and arranged to meet the following week. After I put the phone down I felt guilty about not arranging to see him right away. It wasn't like I had any time to spare. I ended up eating way too much over that weekend – mindful eating got completely forgotten about. I justified this excess as my last chance to party before getting strict on my diet. Of course this foolishness meant that not only had I less time to lose the weight, but I also had more weight to lose.

I'd arranged to meet Brad in Seacon Square. This is one of the huge shopping malls that are spread across Bangkok. I'd worked there briefly in a private school where I'd taught conversational English to a group of Thai business people. That had been one of my first jobs in Thailand almost a decade earlier. I'd also been to Seacon Square a few times in recent months to bring my son to visit Yoyo land; a large amusement park on the top floor of the centre.

I arrived in the prearranged meeting spot a few minutes early. I'd asked the guys in the gym for Brad's description, and they reckoned he was impossible to miss. He had been a former Mr Universe, or had won some other important muscle building competition, and he was built like an armoured truck. When I walked into Starbucks I immediately saw a guy who fit this description. I walked over and introduced myself.

I ordered a tea and sat down in the chair across from Brad. He had a notebook out and was doing some calculations. He put his homework away and gave me the once over. He asked me what I wanted and this question sort of took me by surprise. I thought that maybe this was some sort of test or maybe this wasn't the right guy after all. Thinking back he never actually said that he was waiting for me; he just didn't look confused when I introduced myself. I had taken that to mean that he was Brad but what if he wasn't?

I explained my situation a bit hesitantly. All the time I kept worrying that this could be the completely wrong guy and that I sounded like a nutcase. What type of weirdo goes up to a stranger in Starbucks and begins talking about their weight problems? It came as a great relief when he once again took out his notebook and began writing notes. Surely he wouldn't be jotting down such information unless he had come to give me nutrition advice?

Brad further allayed my fears of mistaken identity when he restated my problem in a more simplified way. He then went on to promise me that we would have a solution for my weight problems by the end of our session. He would explain exactly what I needed to do, but first of all he was going to have to educate me about the basics of nutrition. I managed to ignore a prideful urge to tell him that I already knew a lot about nutrition. This turned out to be a wise move because by the time that Brad had finished talking it was obvious that I knew very little on the subject.

As Brad began explaining the basics of nutrition he'd occasionally stop to ask me questions about my current diet. He would then go on to clearly explain why my eating habits were wrong. He used funny examples that brought otherwise dry material to life. He referred to the different nutrients as if they were characters in a play; this made it easier for the information to stick in my mind. He wasn't putting this much effort into teaching me about nutrition just for the hell of it. He reminded me more than once that if I could understand the reasons behind healthy eating choices this would make it easier for me to do the right thing.

Brad surprised me with the claim that the source of my problems wasn't the amount that I ate but the way that I ate. I should be consuming a lot more protein if I wanted to have more muscle. I also needed to stop stuffing myself with sugary things before going to bed. This is because if carbohydrate isn't being used for creating energy it gets turned into fat; so eating carbohydrates before going to bed is just asking for trouble. Even eating a lot of fruit in the evening is not a good idea – something I do a lot. He told me that the only food I should be consuming before sleep is protein; my body could use this nutrient to repair itself and build muscle while I slept.

One of the other key elements of Brad's plan for my weight loss involved eating more regularly. At first his suggestion sounded a bit ridiculous; surely eating more would be the last thing I needed to do. He went on to explain how meals every three hours could actually help me burn more calories. My digestive system would need to keep going practically all the time; it would force my body to work harder. He also recommended that I decrease my daily calorie count down to 2,000 a day. I'd still be eating a small meal of 400 calories every three hours so I'd never get hungry.

By the time Brad had finished his nutrition lecture he had me convinced. He'd explained things so well that it all seemed simple and obvious now. I still believed that my ideas about mindful eating were effective, but this new information would give my weight loss attempt a turbo-charge. He warned me that in the beginning my weight might go up, but I should get down to 70kg by the week before the fight. I could then just dehydrate for the weigh-in to lose the final few kilograms – just like Tim had suggested.

The thing I liked most about Brad's advice was that he had not just offered me a quick fix. He had described a new way of dealing with food. If I were to make a few simple, but permanent, changes it should mean that my weight would remain stable in the future. Mindful eating got my weight down to an acceptable level, but these other changes would bring me into the comfort zone of a healthy diet. I still wasn't sure about how eating every three hours would work out, but his conviction had been persuasive, and I already felt convinced. The other changes, like avoiding carbohydrates before going to bed, weren't going to be that much of a hardship.

The only element of this new weight loss plan that worried me was the expectation that I stick to 400 calories a meal. This would be fine during most of the day, but I looked forward to my large meal after I'd finish work. I had reduced the amount I ate at this time as part of my mindful eating project, but this would mean a further reduction. Still, it was going to be a small sacrifice to make if it meant meeting my weight target at the end of a month. Before meeting up with Brad I had been expecting far harsher changes to my diet so I couldn't really complain.

I had reluctantly sought advice from this sports nutrition expert, but his words really did make a huge difference to me. The problem with just using the internet for information is that it is too easy to hear what you want to hear and not what you need to hear. I'm sure there was nothing that this guy told me that I couldn't have found online. He put all the information into context for me and I think that this is the real purpose of experts. Sure it is great that we can now find out almost anything we want with just a few clicks of the keyboard, but without a proper framework this information can be a bit meaningless.

Brad's warning that I might initially put on weight didn't apply in my case. Within the first week of his diet I lost almost 2kg. The weight continued to fall steadily throughout the month of June. I decided to only eat 350 calorie meals most of the time; that way I could still have a largish meal in the evenings. This compromise worked out well, and I didn't miss the 50 calories from each of the other meals.

Chapter 20

TRAINING WITH OTHER PEOPLE MEANT that Muay Thai felt more satisfying to me. I did feel like the class dunce a lot of the time, but none of the other students ever questioned my qualifications. Nobody thought it odd that somebody my age would want to begin training. Not that I had many deep conversations with the other foreigners; mostly it was just a quick "how you doing?" We all tended to get wrapped up in our own little world when we trained. Despite this lack of excessive verbal communication the atmosphere in Sitsongpeenong felt friendly – sort of like we were all on the same team and fighting the same battles.

One of the things I've continued to struggle with since giving up alcohol is handling social situations. I've always had a bit of a problem dealing with other people, and I just feel awkward sometimes. One of the initial things that attracted me to alcohol was that it gave me confidence to speak to strangers. The more I drank the more extroverted I became – especially during those first few years of drinking. Now that alcohol is no longer part of my life I once again feel a bit uncomfortable around people I don't know very well. It is not so much the actual interaction itself, but the negative mental chatter going on inside my brain.

One of the reasons I love writing so much is I find that it is a much easier way for me to communicate with people. When I write things down it gives me the chance to figure out what I'm going to say. I'll often find when writing that the point I'm trying to make isn't worded very well, or that it sounds a bit odd. I have the delete key so the evidence of my flawed passage of thought is erased permanently. If only such a delete key existed with normal conversations, I would never have any problems again.

I find it so much easier to get my point across when I write things down. I can be talking to other people and it feels as if I am drowning; the words coming out of my mouth are not related to my original point. I've lost the thread of what I want to say, but I am trying to bluff my way – it is like I am paddling wildly just to stay afloat. It is usually at this stage that I begin to mumble, and this makes conversation even more difficult. This never happens when I write because I can go back and mess around with the text until it actually says what I mean.

The other difficulty that I have when communicating verbally is that I get excited – this happens a lot. I end up talking way too fast. I used to think that people couldn't understand me because of my Irish accent, but that isn't usually the problem. The real difficulty is my speed and my tendency to mutter when I feel embarrassed. This is one of the huge difficulties I've had with learning the Thai language. I mutter and talk too fast in that language as well. My comprehension of Thai is high, but I much prefer reading or listening to it than speaking it.

It is not that I'm unfriendly to the new people I meet – quite the opposite. All too often I walk away from the conversation feeling like a complete idiot because I've talked way too much. My worst conversational gambits involve saying things that do not even make sense to me; it is like my mouth is working independently of my brain. I also sometimes worry that I'm coming across as a bit self-obsessed – I realise that I've been talking for ten minutes and it has all been me, me, me. It is then that I wish for a delete key or at least a rewind button.

I soon found out that training at Sitsongpeenong meant having to constantly meet new people. Every time I turned up there would be at least a couple of new foreigners at the gym. Some of these people only came to train for a few days before doing a bit of travelling around South East Asia. Only a small minority of them stayed longer than a month. Keeping track of the newcomers turned out to be impossible so there were many who came and went without even sharing a hello.

I've learnt to be cautious when meeting other foreigners here in Thailand. Most of the expats are friendly enough when you get to know them, but there are some who would prefer to be left alone. I have a tendency to smile when I make eye contact with strangers – it is something that is almost instinctive. I see it as a friendly gesture and certainly don't mean any harm by it. As far as I know I've always done the same, and it never led to any problems until I moved to Thailand. I've not had a negative reaction from a Thai, as they tend to naturally smile at strangers as well, but with other foreigners this has gotten me into trouble quite a few times. They can react to a friendly smile as if I had begun stalking them; maybe they believe that if they return the smile I will take this as the green light to move in with them.

At first I put the bad reaction to my smile as being due to meeting people when they were having a bad day. After it happened a few times I wondered if the problem might actually be me. Maybe something had happened to my smile, and it now looked like a sneer; it might even look menacing. It was only after I became a bit more involved with the online expat community that I found out that this is a common problem. There really are a lot of foreigners here who hate to be acknowledged in any way by other foreigners. So the problem wasn't my smile only that I was directing it at the wrong people.

THE MOST USUAL WAY THAT such people react to the unrequested smile in their direction is to just stare blankly back at me. I still can't help but feel a tiny bit offended when this happens; sort of like I've put my hand out and the other person has refused to shake it. Still this type of slight is water off a duck's back, and it is quickly forgotten about. Some Westerners will react to the smile with a look of complete contempt – occasionally even an angry "tut". I remember one guy in particular who just spat the word 'farang' (the Thai word for white foreigner) in my direction like a curse; clearly forgetting that he too shared the same label in the eyes of a Thai.

I do understand that just because other people

have the same skin colour (I've only ever noticed this negative reaction coming from white Westerners) as me it doesn't mean we are related or that we should be friends – to think that would be just crazy. In reality I haven't actually singled out any of these people for special attention. I'm not trying to befriend them or get them into a conversation – usually the last thing I want is to stop for a chat. I'm just giving a friendly acknowledgement like I do to everyone else I make eye contact with – no big deal.

For over five years I lived in a rural part of Thailand where there were only two other Westerners living within a ten kilometre radius. I remember the first time meeting one of these guys at the weekly market. I gave him a friendly smile, but he just returned the blank stare. We were always bumping into each other after that, but there was never any acknowledgement of each other's existence. Oa couldn't understand the reason for this behaviour, and I couldn't really explain it myself. Deliberately not acknowledging somebody involves a lot of hard work, and it hardly seems worth it. The weekly market would be the highlight of the week in this part of rural Thailand. I enjoyed it less because of my bizarre relationship with this other foreigner.

I adapted to these unsatisfying encounters by attempting to control my natural inclination to smile. I'd wait for them to acknowledge me first before I'd do the same. This made such encounters unnecessarily uncomfortable. I felt like a gunslinger at high noon waiting for his opponent to draw. Sometimes I would be too late acknowledging a smile and I'd feel bad about it; now I was being unfriendly. Other times I'd wrongly anticipate a positive acknowledgment only to be faced with a blank stare – tricky fucker!

I later progressed to avoiding eye contact with foreigners as much as possible. This wasn't too difficult when I lived in rural Thailand. I only tended to bump into other Westerners when I went shopping in Phitsanulok city. I'd end up playing a type of supermarket chess where I'd avoid going down aisles if I noticed another foreigner lurking there. It could sometimes require a great deal of strategy to get my shopping done without such a confrontation. I'd have to plan ahead to predict where the other guy would go next. It felt pathetic and stupid but at least it solved the whole smile or not to smile dilemma.

The Westerners who arrive at Sitsongpeenong for the most part are friendly. There can be the odd one who comes across as a bit of a cold fish. I suppose that it shouldn't really come as any surprise to find that Muay Thai attracts a lot of macho people; those who want to be respected as tough guys. When these individuals first come to the camp they have something to prove; they can strut around like one of those male peacocks that like to show off their feathers to the competition. For the first few days they can come across as unfriendly and deadly serious. They tend to lighten up a bit after that; I suspect because they feel they have already proved themselves and found their place in the pecking order.

It felt a bit strange to be training with people who were so tough and aggressive. The weirdest thing of all was how they just seemed to accept me. I felt like a young kid who had been allowed to play with the grownups. I felt honoured to be admitted into this strange world of tough guys. I was training right alongside career fighters – skilled athletes who had managed to turn their bodies into fighting machines and made a living from it. It took me a bit of time to realise it but quite a few of my fellow students were stars in the world of Muay Thai. People like Kem Sitsongpeenong (many of the top Thai fighters use the name of their camp as their surname) who was a world welterweight champion. Nobody ever said to me, "hey, you're one of us", but they never said I wasn't and this felt almost as good.

So despite my sometimes flawed interpersonal skills I did enjoy meeting people at Sitsongpeenong. I continued to have conversations that left me feeling like an idiot afterwards, but there were also times when it felt like I'd found my tribe.

The mood of the gym changed with the people; sometimes the tension felt like a physical thing in the air. I wasn't attending the regular classes long before I realised that the mood in the gym could shift rapidly. People would be happily talking to me one minute but then they would completely ignore me the next. Given my tendency to narcissism I would assume that I'd done something to irritate them. I would search my memories for any possible reason for such coolness, but I would usually be unable to find an explanation. Of course these mood changes had nothing to do with me – at least most of the time anyway.

When people train full-time at Muay Thai they will have good days and bad days – mood can even change significantly over the course of one session. Preparing for combat is tough; it plays havoc with the emotions. I had expected Muay Thai to be a physical challenge, but it took me awhile to realise that the real challenge is mental. People get absorbed in their own internal preparations; it can be like other individuals in the gym cease to exist. The mood fluctuations become more severe as people get nearer to a fight. Sometimes they give up a vibe that says "keep the fuck away from me". Despite the real atmosphere of camaraderie in the camp, Muay Thai combat involves a journey that people need to make alone.

When I saw how the fight preparations affected other people mentally it worried me a lot. I'd expected that fighters would be nervous before stepping into a ring, but I hadn't realised how intense these feelings could be. I noticed one guy who began acting particularly strangely in the days before his fight – he started to talk to himself and appeared to be hallucinating at times. He was experiencing some type of nervous breakdown due to the stress of his preparations. He went on to win his encounter and his behaviour returned to normal afterwards.

Watching these people put themselves through so much stress only further emphasised the strangeness of this desire to fight. If people were to do the same thing outside of the ring then there is a good chance that at least one of them would end up in jail. Being hit by another person is about as personal as you can get. In a full-contact fighting sport like Muay Thai you are more or less giving another person permission to try and kill you. Even one blow from a skilled Nak Muay could be enough to cause death. So when people sign up to fight they are agreeing to put their life in danger – there is no doubt about that. In reality relatively few people die as a result of these bouts but only because the art also involves being able to absorb and defend against blows.

In some ways this inner urge that humans have to fight as a sport seems to be against our survival instincts. But then again the same could be said about lots of other things as well such as skydiving or climbing the Himalayas. There is just something so appealing about living on the edge. I guess the real reason for why humans like to fight like this is that it is still part of our nature. Most of us no longer have to fight to survive, but this instinct is still there driving us.

Many of us learn to ignore this urge to fight – fear keeps it at bay. Instead we opt for a safe life as much as we can. We satisfy these urges vicariously via TV and movies. It is the real risk takers that we admire the most; those who are willing to put their life in danger just for the thrill of it. I'm not sure that it is possible to become successful at anything in life without taking at least some risks. I know from personal experience that my own life didn't really start to take off until I began to take more chances. In order to become a writer I had to get over my fear of being rejected.

Chapter 21

THE TRANSITION TO FULL-TIME TRAINING went smoothly enough. I'd been warned by other people in the camp that I was at risk of picking up injuries if I didn't give my body a chance to acclimatise to the increased intensity. In the week before turning full-time I'd managed to make it to the gym every day for the afternoon session. I also trained each morning at home. I felt the fittest I'd ever been in my life and the last bit of stomach fat had almost disappeared. I was bursting with energy a lot of the time. Sometimes it felt that despite the many hurdles I still had to overcome I was being taken towards my first encounter in the ring by an unstoppable force – it would all work out somehow. I felt excited and privileged to have an opportunity to train full-time.

Khru Jack no longer stuck me on the stationary bike for warm up. I was allowed to skip with the rest of the class. I struggled a bit in the beginning but now had no problem completing 30 minutes continuous skipping. My technique left a lot to be desired, but I preferred to skip instead of using the old man bike – it felt a bit manlier.

I'd heard from other people that the key to a successful first fight is good conditioning – train hard and fight easy. I doubted that much could be done to improve my fighting skills too significantly within a few weeks, but I felt confident that my physical conditioning would be good enough by the time the big day arrived. This was one part of the training that I could control; the fear of being hurt in the ring would motivate me to train at maximum intensity.

I made a decision to just follow any instructions given to me by the trainers. This meant having faith that they wouldn't try to push me beyond my limits. I made a pledge that during any training exercise I would keep going until they told me to stop. This willingness to do whatever it took had worked for me before. This had been the attitude that I took with me when I went to Thamkrabok to escape my alcohol addiction. I swore then that I would do whatever the monks told me to do. If they had wanted me to run naked around Thailand I would have done it. This type of humility ensured that I did what was necessary, and it put me in the right frame of mind to learn. Hopefully the same attitude would pay dividends now.

Maybe I wouldn't be prepared to run naked around Thailand, but I would put 100% into the training. I would prove to everyone that I was ready to fight, and not just some blow-hard that wanted to write a book. I'd built up my fitness level in recent months so felt that my body could now withstand a lot of abuse. The more stamina I could rely on in the fight the better it would be for me. Fitness would be the only real advantage that I could have over my opponent. I just couldn't imagine that there would be anyone with as low a skill set as mine that would be willing to fight.

I didn't have to wait long before my decision to just obediently follow the instructions of the trainers got put to the test. On this particular day we had a new trainer at Sitsongpeenong; I say 'trainer', but I have no real idea what his credentials were. I have not seen him in the gym since that day. Maybe he had just been some guy off the street who happened to like bossing people around. In Thailand it is perfectly feasible that a stranger could walk into in a Muay Thai class and start helping out; especially with foreign students. The Thais would be unlikely to tell him to "piss off" because of the fear of causing a loss of face. It would be a delicate situation and so the most likely response would be to leave the intruder to run out of steam.

My encounter with this man occurred while I was practising my knee technique up and down the outside of the ring. He came over to give me some pointers. He smelled badly of alcohol and his eyes had the shiny glow of somebody still intoxicated; given my personal history I didn't judge him too harshly for this. What did bother me was that he insisted that I copy his version of the knee kick. He had an odd way of doing things; I suspected that a key element of his technique required at least a bit of drunkenness. He spent a good 15 minutes trying to get me to copy his movements. I dutifully obeyed but felt relieved when he left; I automatically went back to the way I'd been shown by the regular teachers.

On the last Saturday before beginning full-time training I attended my first morning session. I had been looking forward to this because it was a part of life at the camp that I'd not yet experienced. The foreigners at Sitsongpeenong are expected to be running in the park by 6am; the Thais start half an hour earlier than this. I would have to leave the house at about 5.15am to be sure to make it to the park on time. I'm normally up and working at the computer by 5am anyway so getting out of bed wasn't such a big deal for me.

Suang Luang is a park just a short distance away from Sitsongpeenong. This is where the Nak Muay do their running except on those days when it is raining – then they just do laps around the ring in the gym. I had to drive past the park in order to get to Sitsongpeenong, but I'd never bothered to go inside. My mother, wife, and son had visited Suang Luang a couple of weeks before while I trained at the gym – they managed to have a pleasant afternoon there. I never ventured any further than the car park to drop them off and pick them up; I reasoned that I would have plenty of time to get to know the park later.

Suang Luang turned out to be much bigger than I'd expected. I had not bothered to ask for precise instructions about where to run because I just assumed it would be obvious – it wasn't and I couldn't see anyone from the gym. I'd heard some of the other guys talking about some loop around a lake where they would train, but I had no idea where that was. The only thing for it was to just get running in the hope that I'd bump into somebody familiar.

I found running on tarmac with shoes on to be surprisingly hard work; more demanding than running barefoot around the outside of my house. I could feel myself getting tired after just ten minutes, but I kept on going. Almost 30 minutes had gone by before I bumped into Khru Jack; he was on the other side of the park. I then noticed some of the Thai fighters running on a path around a lake. This was obviously the loop that everyone had been talking about.

It took about seven minutes to do a loop of the lake. There were a couple of trainers keeping an eye on things and offering encouragement as needed. The fact that the path went around the lake meant that the trainers could easily see when people were slacking off; there was nowhere to hide.

At 50 minutes into the run I'd had enough; I couldn't imagine running for one more minute. I felt relieved to see that a couple of the other Westerners had already stopped and were walking back in the direction of the gym. I began slowing down as I approached the small bridge which would bring me to the car park and the chance to sit down for a couple of minutes. Khru Jack spotted me before I could make my escape and ordered me to do one more lap.

It felt a bit unfair that I should be expected to keep running after everyone else had stopped, but I remembered my promise to do whatever the trainers told me to do. I managed one more lap around the lake, and even sprinted the last few metres. My sudden burst of enthusiasm went unnoticed as even Khru Jack had abandoned the park by this stage.

I'd parked my car in the Suang Luang so I got to drive the few hundred metres to the gym – as soon as I sat down behind the wheel my body began to issue complaints. I already felt exhausted and couldn't imagine how I was now going to be able to manage a full Muay Thai session. I thought about just driving home and not bothering with the morning session at all; maybe just doing the run would be sufficient this time. Then I remembered how little time I had left to get ready for the fight. I did my best to appear enthusiastic as I limped up the stairs to the training area.

I'd expected a few minutes reprieve before the training began, but this wasn't how it worked at all. As soon as I walked through the door Jack told me to put on my wraps for pad work. I dutifully obeyed even though my legs felt like lumps of concrete. The next five rounds on the pads weren't as challenging as I would have expected. The pace wasn't too strenuous. Somewhere around the third round I got a second wind, and I actually began to enjoy myself.

After the pad work I spent 20 minutes practising on the bags. A trainer would occasionally come over to offer advice on my technique, but there was nobody shouting at me to be more active. I'd heard that the morning sessions were a bit more laid back, and it did seem to be the case. There were only two other foreigners training this morning and when they disappeared Khru Jack decided that there would be no clinching that session. I felt a bit guilty about feeling so relieved when he said this.

I also attended the Saturday afternoon session to make this the first day of full-time training. I made the most of my break in-between. I went to bed for an hour. I actually felt quite refreshed for the second session of the day. This turned out to be another relaxed affair as none of the other foreigners turned up; they were all too busy getting ready to enjoy a night on the town. At the end of the session Khru Jack decided that he wanted to clinch with me. I enjoyed this as he spent the whole time offering advice on what I should be doing. It was the first time that I really felt comfortable clinching; mostly because he deliberately made the whole thing easy for me. I even managed to throw him onto the ring floor a couple of times, and this brought cheers from the other trainers. It worked to boost my confidence, and I began to consider the possibility that I might one day clinch competently.

The next day was Sunday and my final day off before going full-time at Muay Thai. I'd hoped to do something nice with my wife and son. I would not have much time to go anywhere once intensive training got underway. This could be our last chance for a family day for a few weeks. When the day arrived I was too exhausted to do anything. I ended up just watching movies on the computer; a complete waste of a Sunday, but every part of my body felt stiff and in pain.

Chapter 22

On Monday morning it was back to Suan Luang for the morning run. This time I parked the car at the gym and walked back to the lake. A group of the Thai fighters were already running. They were on the other side of the lake, but I recognised the Sitsongpeenong shorts. I kept my own pace and fell into a nice rhythm. No trainer had arrived yet in the park so there were no calls to speed things up. The morning felt nice and cool and this is always a blessing when you live in Bangkok. I experienced a surge of positivity; it just felt so healthy to be up at dawn and running around this park.

I ran past quite a few people who were practising Tai Chi. Some of these early risers looked to be in their seventies yet they were moving with impressive agility. I even noticed a few Westerners practising this ancient martial art. One of them was wearing a Kung Fu outfit and had a blue sash around his head – this seemed a little over the top. His movements were graceful though, so I could easily forgive his little eccentricity.

Watching these people practise Tai Chi reminded me of how much I missed it. I still would occasionally try to do the short-form at home, but I'd forgotten a lot. I know that Tai Chi can be an effective martial art, but I tend to see it more as a type of moving meditation with health benefits. I try to keep an open mind on the subject of chi energy, but even if this turns out to be fanciful nonsense there is no doubt that there are some important health benefits related to these movements. I only had to look at these older people practicing in the park to see that.

As well as those practising morning Tai Chi there were also plenty of other health conscious folk in the park that morning. The majority were walking or doing a combination of walking with the occasional brief burst of jogging. Almost everyone wore sports apparel. I also noticed a group of people doing an aerobic workout that seemed quite intense. I felt a great sense of comradeship with these other people. Like me, they had left their beds early so that they could focus on physical fitness. Most of them were smiling and seemed happy to be in the park on such a beautiful morning. I would not have been surprised if everyone had suddenly broken into song.

Other than martial arts I would have to say that walking is my favourite way to keep fit. One thing that I regret about living in Thailand is that I hardly ever walk anywhere. I blame the heat for this and the lack of footpaths in many areas. My wife never realised that people liked to walk for fun until she visited Ireland. It just isn't something that people do a lot of in Thailand – at least not on the roads and streets anyway. When I first moved to a rural part of Phitsanulok I did try to start walking in the evenings, but it didn't work out. I got pissed off because every couple of minutes (literally) somebody would stop to offer me a lift on their motorbike or on their tractor. No matter how many times I told them "okk gamlang gai," they just could not get their head around somebody walking along the road for exercise.

Even during my years as an alcoholic I would walk a lot. My favourite thing to do in London was to go on a solo pub crawl on my day off. I would walk from one area of the city to another and see how many pubs I could manage along the way. I would even sometimes get it into my head that I needed to see the countryside, or to be more precise to have a few drinks in a country pub. I would keep walking out towards the suburbs of London until I hit farmland. Once I walked 37 miles in such an attempt. By the end of the day I would be practically crawling; a combination of tiredness as well as drunkenness. I never told many people about these adventures at the time because they would probably have accused me of insanity.

Somehow I'd not considered the Bangkok parks as a place for me to exercise. It should have been obvious, but it just had never entered my thinking. All that time complaining about lack of exercise opportunities when the solution was so obvious. Maybe if I had considered this option I would not have allowed myself to become such a slob – probably wishful thinking. I could see now that going to somewhere like Suang Luang in the mornings or evenings provided the perfect conditions for walking or running.

I did a lot of long-distance running in my teens. I took it up originally because I wanted to improve my physical conditioning for Kung Fu. When I first started entering sparring competitions I would feel knackered after a couple of rounds. One of the trainers suggested

PAUL GARRIGAN

that I probably needed to build up my cardiovascular endurance. I'd also read how Bruce Lee had liked to run for an hour every morning. I began running as a way to increase my stamina and to be more like Bruce Lee. In the end it didn't make much difference to my performance in competitions, but I kept running because I enjoyed it so much.

One of the things I loved so much about running during those years was that I felt no pressure to impress anybody. In the beginning I didn't run with anyone else so I just set my own pace; I would feel free to enjoy the experience. Martial arts meant so much to me that I was always putting pressure on myself to perform better. That need to impress wasn't there with running.

I walk a bit like a duck with my two feet pointing outwards. It isn't that big a deal. I had worried that my funny feet would interfere with my ability to run, but it wasn't a problem at all. Running just felt natural and almost effortless. I would get up early in the morning and run for an hour before going to school. I did this even during the coldest days of winter.

This was the early '80s and jogging had just become hugely popular in Ireland. The first Dublin City Marathon took place in 1980, and it really caught the public's imagination. There seemed to be distance races taking place every other week. I hadn't even considered entering one because I had enough on my plate with Kung Fu.

My aunty Pauline had developed the running bug, and she had already completed the Dublin Marathon. She suggested that I enter a 10K race that was going to be taking place in Bray, a nearby town. She would also be running. I didn't do any extra training, but I still performed quite well on the day. I completed it in just under the 40 minute mark, and even won a pair of Kangaroo running shoes for my efforts. The nicest thing about the race though, was how relaxed I felt throughout. I just got into a rhythm and this took me effortlessly past so many other runners in that race; I wasn't really competing against them in my mind.

I competed in another 10K a few months later; this road race took place in the local hills where I did most of my running. I managed to put in another 40 minute performance, but there was no prize this time. For some reason I never ran competitively again after this. I never made a conscious decision not to compete anymore. I had hoped to train for the Dublin City Marathon but my father managed to talk me out of this, I was still only 14. He worried that running too much would damage my growing bones. When I gave up martial arts a year later I also stopped running. Over the next couple of decades I did try to rekindle my interest in running, but like martial arts it never fully took hold. I'd run for a few weeks, but then give up on it.

As I ran around Suan Luang that morning I remembered all the reasons why I'd once enjoyed this activity so much. I even had flash backs of the runs in my teens; those cold winter mornings when I'd feel so cosy inside my tracksuit. So much had happened in the intervening years, but somehow I felt closer to my younger self. I also thought of my dad and how he would surely be proud to see me now – more proof that I had managed to get my life back on track.

The first week of full-time training was now

underway. My life for the next few weeks would revolve almost completely around Muay Thai. I would be pushing myself harder than I'd ever done in the past. This time I could not afford to hold anything back because that could spell disaster in the ring. For most of my life my policy had been to avoid giving my best; that way if I failed there would be the consolation of knowing that my efforts had not been 100%. This time I had to give my all so if I failed there would be no such consolation. I had never faced a test where there was so much to lose.

Much of the credit for my current fitness level had to go to Khru Jack. He pushed me hard and knew my limits a lot better than I did. Some of the other foreigners would complain that he didn't pay enough attention to technique, but his actions were deliberate. He took care of the newbies in the gym. It was his job to get them in good physical shape. Once they had passed satisfactorily through his hands they would then be ready to move to a trainer who focused more on the technical side of things. Without reaching this high level of physical fitness with Khru Jack they would not be able to get the most from the other trainers.

Over the previous few months I'd seen how other students would stay with Khru Jack for a week or two until they were in good shape. They would then be reassigned to another instructor. My graduation day never arrived. I almost always trained with Khru Jack. It was like he had taken me on as a pet project and wanted to see things through until the end. I had mixed feelings about this. I respected him a great deal as a teacher, but I also wanted a chance to learn from somebody else – someone who would be more focused on my techniques. It came as a relief then to find that on my second day of full-time training I was assigned to another teacher; at least for the pad work anyway.

My new instructor didn't push me as hard as Khru Jack, but the session still turned out to be physically more demanding. I'd become so used to training with Khru Jack that I could usually predict the technique he would want me to do next before he even opened his mouth – this made it easy for me to go into autopilot. I'd be moving fast but the pattern would be predictable so not too much of a challenge. With this new guy he tried to keep me moving as if we were in an actual fight. I had no idea what technique he was going to demand next, and to make things even more difficult he would randomly attack me to check my defences. Khru Jack did this sometimes too, but he tended to give a warning just before his attack. Khru Ton tended to only attack when I let my guard down. With this new guy I had to be prepared to defend at all times; just like I'd have to be in a real fight.

Despite a bit of exhaustion I felt great at the end of this session on the pads. The trainer had pointed out quite a few flaws in my techniques, but they all appeared to be things that would be easy to fix. I didn't move my standing leg to the side enough when hurling out a turning kick, but once he showed me how exactly I was doing it wrong it felt natural to do things the right way. My punches were also a bit ineffective because my fist moved upwards at the last moment of a strike; this too could be easily remedied. After the pads I went to the bags and practised the amendments to the techniques that I'd just been shown.

I expected there to be a bit of clinching at the end of the session, but when I went to take off my wraps Khru Jack stopped me. He wanted me to spar instead. I felt like a deer trapped in the headlights of a car. I knew that some sparring experience would be crucial, but now that we were actually about to get down to it I had to fight against the urge to refuse. There were no other foreigners in the gym again that day so I worried about who I would be expected to fight; I just hoped that he didn't plan to put me up against one of the Thai fighters. I felt shaky as I put on the large 18 ounce gloves and leg pads. I felt a bit calmer once I saw that Khru Jack was also putting on the big gloves.

The couple of rounds of sparring were relaxed and Khru Jack hardly tried to hit me at all. Despite this laid back introduction I still managed to perform disappointingly; once again I found that hitting pads or bags is not the same as hitting another person. To make matters worse I'd selected a dodgy leg guard that would not tie behind my leg properly. Every time that I went to kick with my right leg the pad would come off, and I'd need to retie it. Even with this excuse my performance could best be described as a bit dismal. Khru Jack easily managed to evade every attack I launched, and every time he so much as lifted his leg I'd go into panic mode. I'd already accepted that I'd no natural talent for clinching, but I had been rather hoping to at least show some aptitude for sparring.

I tried to ignore the reality that the expectation of

moving from my current level of sparring inexperience to a professional fight in a few weeks could be described as insanely optimistic. The only conceivable outcome would be getting badly beaten in the ring. Even during those times when it felt like some higher force was guiding me towards this fight, I couldn't believe that this would prevent me from losing and at least picking up some minor injuries. I felt guilty because not only did I intend to risk my own health but also my family's future. Did I really have the right to be so reckless?

I knew that an amateur Muay Thai fight would be a much better option for me. At least that way I would get to wear some protective pads on my head and shins during the fight. There would also be rules banning the particularly dangerous strikes such as elbows. Nak Muay in Europe and America got their introduction into competitive fighting that way. It would not even be possible for someone of my level to enter anything other than an amateur fight back in the West. Such competitions were not popular in Thailand. I knew that a couple of the foreigner-focused gyms in Phuket offered amateur fights with protection, but it just wouldn't be feasible to go there to train and fight. The only competitions that Sitsongpeenong had to offer me would be proper professional bouts.

The other option open to foreign Muay Thai fighters just looking for a bit of glory in the ring would be to go up against a taxi driver. There were usually people who no longer trained but would be willing to fight if they got paid for it. The great benefit of fighting these individuals would be that they had no real desire to win; they would also usually be out of shape physically. This meant that any foreigner – with a bit of conditioning – would have no problem winning against them. I definitely didn't want to fight an opponent who would let me win for money. I would feel like a fraud, and there would be no sense of achievement. The only option then seemed to be a professional fight even though there would be a good chance of being seriously injured.

Chapter 23

AT THE NEXT SESSION AT Sitsongpeenong I had another opportunity to spar; this time against proper opponents. The bit of sparring with Khru Jack had been an easy introduction, but now I couldn't expect such accommodating opposition. This time there would be real blows being exchanged, and I would have to suck at least some of them up. I knew that we were expected to take it easy when sparring but I already knew from the clinching that some people had a very liberal idea of what 'taking it easy' actually meant. For some of them anything short of knocking their opponent out could be considered taking it easy.

I felt like a condemned man as I put on the heavy gloves and leg pads. I would finally be getting the sparring practice I so sorely needed, but this did not seem so important now. When I worked as a nurse I accompanied many of my patients to the operating theatre. Like them I knew that what lay ahead was likely to benefit me, but it didn't mean that I had to like it. I tried to look confident as I climbed back into the ring, but my reluctance must have been obvious. My facial expressions always give away my internal conditions; the slight tremor in my body would have also been a huge giveaway. For a couple of crazy seconds I worried that I might burst into tears.

Khru Jack had two opponents waiting for me inside the ring. We were to take turns fighting for four minute sessions. He wanted us to go for six rounds like this; two of us fighting and one resting. I'd only ever done a couple of rounds of very light sparring so this sounded like a ridiculously ambitious plan but refusing did not feel like an option to me. If I planned to fight in a few weeks I needed to get sparring experience right away. I also knew that my inability to face sparring now would mean that there would be no way that I would later summon the courage to step into the ring for real. I just had to do this.

The first round saw me up against a French guy. Marcus had been training at Sitsongpeenong for a couple of weeks. I'd gotten to speak to him for the first time that morning during the run. He spoke perfect English due to living in the United States for many years. Marcus had a lot of experience in Muay Thai and had entered a few professional fights back in the West. He'd managed to win a few of these encounters, but had failed to make it into the big time. Marcus confided in me that he had come to Thailand for what he saw as his last chance to find success as a fighter. He seemed to be a naturally friendly guy with a good sense of humour, I liked him.

I felt a bit surprised to be matched up against Marcus in my first sparring session. He was in a completely different league than me technically. I only had to see him train for a few minutes to know that. He also outweighed me by at least 30kg; in his case this was mostly muscle and not fat. I'd hoped to be introduced to sparring by going up against somebody my own level. I doubted that this match-up would be much fun for my opponent either. He surely had not travelled all the way across the world to fight somebody at my level of expertise; I would have expected him to be training with the Thai fighters. Maybe the trainers thought that it would be better to throw me in at the deep end. I worried that they just weren't thinking at all. I just hoped that my opponent appreciated my skill level and would be willing to make allowances for me.

I faced Marcus in the ring. The gum shield gave him a menacing look. I offered him a friendly smile to try and ease the tension, but he didn't return it. It was like he was looking through me. My stress levels rose significantly as I could already tell that this wasn't going to be a comfortable few minutes for me. We were told to start fighting, and I reluctantly began to move towards my opponent. I gave a tentative jab in his direction that never had any chance of hitting him. He responded by landing about five punches on me. They were all hard and they all hurt me. All I could do was lower my head beneath my guard and wait for the hail of punches to end.

I felt stunned by the aggression of Marcus's attack. His power let me know that he definitely wanted to hurt me. One of the blows to the side of my head had left me reeling; I struggled to keep my arms up. I looked in Jack's direction as he was there to referee the fight. I expected him to tell Marcus to calm down a bit; to take it easy on the beginner, but the teacher didn't seem in the least bit concerned with the proceedings. I was still reeling from the first attack when Marcus came at me again. I had my hands up to my face to protect against the jab, but it still managed to cause pain. His next hook landed hard and I could feel my legs turning to jelly. I felt afraid; even if I just stayed hidden behind my guard he could still hurt me at will.

I launched a turning kick just to try to keep Marcus at a distance. He responded by kicking my other leg from under me. I hit the ground with a wallop as the air got pushed out of my body. I did not see the sweep coming; I just ended up with my arse on the floor of the ring. I felt winded. He stood above me bouncing on his toes; obviously impatient for me to get up so that he could continue pummelling me. I got to my feet and just went back to hiding behind my guard. I would put out the occasional jab but each time I'd pay for it with hook punches to my head.

His strikes continued to rock me, but I began to feel a bit numb to them. I still felt afraid. Most of all I worried that one of his blows would do serious damage. The idea of looking like a loser in the ring no longer bothered me; survival instinct had kicked in. I just couldn't understand why this other person was trying so hard to hurt me. I kept on trying to smile at him – I must have looked like a complete idiot. He had no interest in my attempts at friendliness, and his intensity never wavered for one second. I couldn't understand him. He obviously knew that he could demolish me; he had already more than proved his superiority. Why was he trying to inflict further pain? What did I ever do to him? He obviously got a kick out of watching me suffering. Before entering the ring I'd believed him to be a friendly guy, but now I judged him to be some type of sadistic fucker.

I made it to the end of the first round and just wanted to run from the ring. For a few seconds I would have gladly left Sitsongpeenong and never come back again – I hated Muay Thai. I had definitely not signed up for this level of abuse. I didn't mind getting hurt in a fair fight, but I had been put up against an opponent who completely outclassed me. I also felt that given Marcus' level of aggression he should not be allowed to spar with beginners. I'd been used as a human punch bag and surely there were better ways of introducing people to sparring.

Khru Jack pushed me back into the centre of the ring against my next opponent; an American called Ted. He had a more relaxed attitude and started the round by just sending a few light jabs in my direction. He caught me with an impressive turning kick to the head, but it didn't hurt because my opponent didn't put any power into it. I knew that if Marcus had managed to get me with the same kick he would have used full force and that would have knocked me unconscious. At least this guy didn't seem to be out to cause me harm for the fun of it. I even managed to hit him with a few kicks and punches; although I suspected that he just allowed me to get some hits in out of pity. By the end of the second round I felt completely exhausted and couldn't hold my arms up. This had probably more to do with an adrenalin dump than physical exertion – the stress had made me so tense that it just burned up my energy.

Khru Jack tried to pair me up against Marcus again, but then thankfully changed his mind at the last minute. He must have realised that it was not my turn. My outward appearance also must have given away my inner conviction that I would not be able to keep going. If the teacher had insisted we fight I would have just refused. I went to climb out of the ring, but Khru Jack shouted at me to stay. I drank some water and waited. I just lay with my back against the ropes. Marcus landed some great shots, but Ted seemed to be able to absorb them and showed no sign of being hurt – a smile never left his face for the whole round. Occasionally Ted would land a hard shot on Marcus, and I would inwardly cheer. I would have been willing to pay good money to see my torturer get the shit kicked out of him. It never happened and when the next round came it was my turn to face Marcus again. This time the trainer wasn't going to allow my exhaustion to get in the way.

The second round with Marcus turned out to be a bit easier than the first; his ferocity did not come as such a surprise this time. He continued to hit me hard and would sweep me every time I lifted my leg, but his strikes lacked the viciousness of the first round; luckily for me he had still not adjusted to training twice a day. The sneer on his face told me that he still wanted to do me damage, but his tiredness meant that he couldn't quite manage it. The clock in the corner of the ring counted down the time incredibly slowly; I hated every second of it.

When the sparring ended I just wanted to get out of the gym as fast as possible. I could barely bring myself to look at Marcus, but he came over to talk to me. He had returned to being friendly and smiley. I wondered if he had some type of multiple personality disorder. It felt so bizarre being conversational with somebody who a few minutes before had been trying to kill me, but I didn't want to show my discomfort. Ted joined us and that eased a bit of the tension.

I'd already told Marcus about my plans to fight at the end of the month. He had just seen me in action and my goal now appeared ridiculous to him. He came right out and told me that there was no way that I was going to be ready to fight in a month. Ted agreed that it would be a huge challenge for me to get ready in time. Marcus warned me that in a real fight the intensity would be ten times greater than what he had just dished out. I doubted this but did not feel in any position to argue.

The two of them continued to discuss my lack of skill. Marcus thought it strange that I had been training at Sitsongpeenong for almost a year and that this has been my first time sparring. He mocked my ambitions to step into the ring given my level of expertise. Ted added that it took some people years of sparring practice before they were ready for a real fight. Marcus admitted that some people were so naturally talented they could step into the ring a lot sooner, but I certainly did not belong to this group of hothouse flowers. In an attempt to salvage at least some dignity I claimed to be willing to do anything to get ready for this fight. Marcus rebutted this by saying that it was foolhardy for me to even consider getting into the ring with so little experience. He felt that there was no possible way that

I could win the fight, but if I trained exceptionally hard over the next month I might walk out of the ring rather than being carried out on a stretcher.

The conversation ended with Marcus promising to spar with me every day for the next month to help get me ready. I'm sure he thought that his offer would be helpful, but he might as well have been promising to kick me in the testicles on a daily basis. I did not want to ever have to face Marcus again in the ring – at least not until I had a lot more sparring experience. As far as I was concerned, the guy had behaved like a fucking psycho.

I didn't feel too much pain getting into my car, but by the time I got home it was like my whole body was one giant ache. I noticed that there was a huge bruise on my right shin. I didn't even remember when that had happened. It most likely came from trying to protect myself from one of Marcus' turning kicks. That has been the one time that I managed to get my leg up in time to defend; this has been more by accident than by skill. I could see by the angry red look of this bruise that later it would hurt a bit; it appeared a lot worse than the damage I'd done with the wet t-shirt.

I watched a couple of episodes of *The Ultimate Fighter* that evening; hoping to rejuvenate my manliness. I noticed the way the personality of some of the fighters on this TV show changed once they got inside the ring. They reminded me of Marcus and this made it a bit easier to understand his eagerness to batter me. It is hard to be 100% certain, but I doubt that his aggression had anything to do with me personally. We had just met, and I couldn't remember doing anything to upset him.

It was more likely that this was just his fighting style. I would later meet other people who spar the same way.

There are many fighters who enjoy a laugh and a joke but once they get inside the ring it is all business – it is their job. Some people fight better when they are unemotional and tactical, but for other people their preferred strategy is just open aggression. From what I'd read so far about Muay Thai both of these approaches can be successful.

Some Muay Thai fighters make themselves hate their opponent for the duration of the fight. I'm pretty sure that was the case with Marcus. He probably saw his worst enemy standing before him. No wonder that he felt willing to attack me so mercilessly. I could see the benefit, but I couldn't imagine that such tactics would work for me in a fight. It is just not in my nature. I'm too neurotic to completely hate somebody enough that I would want to destroy them.

The approach to fighting that I felt would work best for me would be to stay calm and tactical; a million miles away from my recent performance. It came as a disappointment to find that I did not already naturally become calm under fire. I'd sort of hoped that all my years of meditation would have turned me into some type of Jedi knight in the ring. In that fight against Marcus my calmness and concentration had completely deserted me. I'd gone into survival mode – if you can class standing there and allowing another person to wallop the shit out of you survival. I'd been stunned by his attacks but maybe things would have been a lot different if I'd managed to stay calm.

My meditation practice had fallen off in the weeks

before I began training full-time. I found it hard to sit down and be calm. As soon as I'd put my arse on the floor I'd become incredibly antsy and start worrying about the planned fight. By quietening my mind it allowed all the doubts and concerns to bubble to the surface. It got so bad on a couple of occasions that it felt like I was about to have a panic attack. In the end I stopped my formal meditation practice altogether.

This inability to meditate concerned me a great deal because calmness would be the only real advantage I could take into a fight – my secret weapon. I believed that if I could stay calm and defend myself then I should be able to make it through one fight even if my skills weren't that great. How could I develop such a Jedi-like mind in the ring when I couldn't even meditate for a few minutes in the comfort of my own home anymore? I'd believed Muay Thai to be a good compliment to my meditation practice but at the moment they felt incompatible. I knew that taking a break from this practice would be a bad idea, but I didn't seem to have much choice.

Chapter 24

I HAD NOW ENTERED MY second week of full-time training. I felt satisfied with my physical progress; I'd adapted well to the increased intensity of the training. I could now go five rounds on the pads without getting out of breath and skip for 40 minutes without hardly breaking into a sweat. Best of all, I no longer felt like a physical wreck in-between classes. My body had adapted much better than I ever would have expected. So long as I didn't pick up a serious injury there should be nothing to stop me being physically in shape for the fight.

I hit a mental speed bump during the middle of that second week. It felt like a black cloud had descended on my thinking. I used to feel this way a lot during my drinking years, but such dark moods were rare for me in sobriety. It wasn't a deep depression or anything; it just felt like everything had been touched by a bit of greyness. The only explanation I could think of for this dramatic alternation in my mood was chemical changes occurring in my brain because of the intensity of my activity. This dark mood wasn't there all the time, but it kept on returning.

Marcus fell into pace beside me during the morning

run on the Wednesday. I still felt a bit wary of him due to our recent encounter in the ring, but I allowed his friendliness to win me over. He asked me how I was adapting to full-time training. I tried to describe some of my feelings to Marcus. He dismissed my negative mood as perfectly normal – something that goes hand in hand with hard training. He told me that fight preparation is just a job and it isn't meant to be enjoyable. I could understand his point of view, but I couldn't completely agree with him. I had a job that I loved, most of the time. I also did not take up Muay Thai for it to become a source of misery; a sacrifice I made for later glory in the ring. What would be the point in that? I didn't intend to become a professional fighter; I had been attracted to the martial arts training and not so much the sport element of things. I kept my opinions to myself though. I'd already noticed that Marcus got a funny look on his face when people disagreed with him. I didn't want to give him further reasons to hate me the next time I had to face him in the ring.

One thing that certainly wasn't helping my current negative mood was the amount of time I spent stuck in Bangkok traffic jams. I would sit in my car not moving for an average of three hours every day – it drove me crazy sometimes. It wouldn't have been so bad if I didn't go home in between sessions at Sitsongpeenong, but there seemed to be no way around this. I had work to do, and I needed to spend at least some time with my family. Anyway I would've been bored stupid if I spent the whole day in the gym. Those who were staying full-time at Sitsongpeenong can retire to their room during their free time; I would have just been hanging around wasting time.

I've only ever driven a car in Thailand so a lot of the craziness on the roads here appears normal to me. I would no doubt struggle if I had to drive in a country where other drivers actually followed the rules of the road. Bangkok traffic is by far the worst in the country – maybe even the world. People drive around with reckless abandon; especially the motorcyclists. It is rare that I make a trip in my car without almost hitting at least one two-wheeled daredevil. I'm not alone in this because I constantly see other drivers have near misses with these bikes. Before I learnt to drive I went everywhere on a motorbike, but it is only now that I've spent some time behind the wheel of a car that I fully understand how dangerous it is. The number of road accidents in Thailand each year is a national scandal, and over 90% of fatalities are people on motorbikes.

The thing that really bugs me is how many of these crazy motorcyclists have their children on the bike with them. It is bad enough risking your own life but putting a child in such danger is a bit appalling. To make matters worse most of these kids do not wear safety helmets. The parents are obliged to wear a helmet or they pay a fine. So you have the bizarre sight of helmeted adults riding their motorbikes like demented nutcases while their kid hangs on for dear mercy with nothing to protect their heads. Mind you the helmets that most people wear in Thailand are completely useless for protection anyway; they are paper-thin and best used for decorative purposes.

I do try to drive defensively; I know that even one

second of lost concentration could be fatal. I would never be able to forgive myself if I hit somebody with the car; even hitting one of the stray dogs that wander into the middle of the road would be upsetting – of course more so for them than me. This meant that the drive to and from the gym each day would be full of stress. When I wasn't stuck staring at the arse of another car I was doing crazy manoeuvres to avoid killing people. Sometimes I arrived at the gym feeling mentally exhausted from all the drama during the drive there.

I had some audio books to listen to in the car. These did make the journey a bit more tolerable, but I still felt frustrated as I sat there looking at the car in front of me – mentally willing it to move. It would be particularly difficult in the evening when I'd be so tired and just wanted to get home. This would also be when the traffic would be at its worst. One day it took me almost two hours to drive the 20 kilometres home. My respect for Bangkok taxi drivers grew as I realised that this is what they had to put up with each day. I could never do that job – I would eventually crack and just abandon my cab in traffic and never go back to it.

One of the most surprising things about Bangkok is that there is hardly ever any road rage. It is rare for people to even blow their horn in anger. The only incident of this type of behaviour that I've observed in Thailand occurred in Foodland, Pattaya. None of those involved in the event were actually Thai and the rage on this occasion got directed towards me. I managed to accidentally piss off a car park full of other foreigners. While trying to manoeuvre my way out of a tight space

I somehow turned the steering wheel too far; this did something to the car horn because it came on, and I couldn't turn it off again. The other drivers must have thought that I was deliberately sounding my horn in anger; some of them hit their own horns and one of them even gave me the finger. A female expat took a break from putting her shopping in the boot of the car to come over and bang hard on the roof of my car. I've never felt so embarrassed in my life. That day I had to drive through Pattaya city with the horn blasting out constantly; the local people seemed unperturbed by this and only the foreigners gave me angry looks.

I do envy the Thai people their calmness while navigating the Bangkok traffic. I all too often feel like I'm about to have a nervous breakdown; sometimes it gets so bad that I'd just love to pull over to the side of the road and begin hurling stones at other vehicles. No matter how bad the traffic becomes the Bangkokonians keep their cool. Their strategy is noticeably more effective than mine; cursing and thoughts of revenge only makes me grumpy. Thinking about it – perhaps a few hours in a traffic jam directly before my first fight would be a good strategy. I would be sure to build up plenty of aggression, and that would benefit me in the ring.

Chapter 25

My SHIN HAD BEEN BADLY bruised from the sparring session with Marcus. It felt tender to the touch, and this meant that I couldn't kick or block kicks using the right leg. I mentioned it to Khru Jack and he ordered that I shouldn't spar until it had healed. Luckily the bruise only lasted a couple of days. I used an anti-inflammatory cream and this helped to speed up the healing.

By the Friday morning my shin had almost completely recovered. I informed Khru Jack about my readiness to resume sparring. When he once again put me up against Marcus I regretted opening my mouth. I seriously considered just saying no to this pairing, but I didn't want to appear like a coward. I also thought that by facing Marcus again it would give my courage a much needed boost. It did take guts to go back up against somebody who had knocked me about so badly before. If I could do this then getting into the ring for a real fight would be less of a challenge. I didn't feel that frightened as I put on the shin pads and gloves; I just felt a bit doomed and depressed by the inevitability of what was about to happen.

My strategy this time would be to just focus on defence. I'd keep calm and only try to attack him if there seemed to be a good chance of actually making contact. All my attempts to hit him last time had been wild and half-hearted. This time I would be more selective. I had spent a lot of time imagining getting some hard hits on him; even accidently kicking him in the balls. Now that it was time to fight my ideas of revenge were completely abandoned. I didn't want to make him angry. If he went after me so brutally when I had been no threat what would he be like after I'd hurt him?

I went three rounds with Marcus this time; there were only the two of us sparring that day. Once again he demolished me, and I hardly got a glove on him. He swept me every time I tried to kick him and each time I'd hit the mat with a thump. One of his punches hit me so hard that I blacked out for a second, but I didn't hit the ground. Near the end of the final round he hit me hard with a turning kick right into the ribs. I knew right away that he had done some damage but managed to hang on for the last few minutes. Once again I hated his guts, but once again I tried to put on a friendly face. At the end of the fight I complimented him on his skills, but his mindset seemed to be still in the, 'I'm going to kill you' mode. He just sneered at me.

I came back for the afternoon session, but the pain in my rib area kept on increasing. I had to excuse myself from clinching after only a couple of seconds. My opponent just tapped the left rib area gently with his knee, but I almost collapsed with the pain. I then tried to do some sit-ups but the discomfort made this impossible. In the end I just took an early shower and went home.

By the time I got to bed that night the rib pain had increased significantly; just lying down felt torturous. I couldn't find a comfortable position in the bed. Every time I turned I'd let out an involuntary whimper. I gave up on sleep at about 2 am, and decided to go online instead. I turned to my trusted medical advisor and Google had plenty to say about rib pain.

I didn't know if my ribs were broken or bruised. From what I could see on the web there didn't seem to be much difference between the two – at least when it came to treatment anyway. It could take a few weeks for the pain to resolve. During that time I would need to protect the ribs so that they would heal. I could already see that this was going to put a limit on what I could do at the gym. Most significantly of all it would mean no sparring or clinching. I felt desperate and clung onto the hope that maybe my ribs hadn't even been bruised. Or maybe I would be able to heal a lot faster than normal people. Both of these hopes turned out to be widely optimistic.

Despite my lack of sleep I made it to the morning run at Suan Luang. My ribs ached when I coughed or laughed, but running wasn't too uncomfortable. Back in the gym I felt like a bit of a wreck, but I made it through the pad work. There was a twinge every time I kicked but nothing too bad. One of the trainers offered to give me a massage while the others were sparring. He'd noticed my lack of effort that morning and put it down to low energy. I explained about my ribs and inability to sleep the night before. He felt sure a massage with Nam Muay would do me good. I'd seen the Thai fighters get these rubs so I felt curious about the effectiveness of the treatment. I'd even bought a bottle of the stuff months before but hadn't opened it because I wasn't sure how to use it.

My masseur told me to lie on my stomach. This made my rib pain worse, but I obeyed in the hope that it might make me feel a bit better. I always end up enjoying massages, but I tend to avoid them as I'm not that keen on being touched by strangers. In reality it isn't actually being touched that is the problem but more the thought of it. I'm always grateful for a massage afterwards and promise myself to have them more regularly. They are just so relaxing. I somehow forget this promise and go back to thinking that I don't like to be touched – strange how my mind works.

The trainer began rubbing the Nam Muay ointment into my body. My shoulders began to burn as he massaged the solution deep into the muscle there. He moved methodologically from one part of my body to the next – setting fire to each area as he went. I doubted such discomfort could possibly be benefiting me in any way, but I tried to just keep still in the hope that it would all be over soon. It was only when he tried to rub the ointment into my damaged rib area that I protested. He agreed to skip that part of my body. At the end I thanked him out of politeness and tried not to look overly eager to get to the shower. I hoped that the water would wash the ointment off and stop the burning, but it actually caused it to intensify. It was only as I walked back to my car that I noticed how awake and full of energy I felt – great stuff that Nam Muay.

It took me a few more sessions to accept that my ribs were going to take weeks rather than days to heal.

I would not be sparring or clinching for the rest of the month. This meant my plans were screwed because there could be no fight without more experience of each of these. I felt despondent as there did not seem to be much point in continuing with full-time training. I really didn't want to give up now though. I had developed momentum, and my physical fitness was climbing to unknown levels. I wanted to know how much higher I could go. It just felt wrong to stop after coming so far.

There was only one solution that would allow me to continue with the project. It was going to be financially hard, but I would need to train full-time for longer than the planned month. Maybe if I could arrange an additional three weeks then it would be enough. The more I thought about it the more sense it made. It would mean that my ribs would have a few weeks to heal, and I'd still have time to get in some sparring and clinching practice. I would also have all those extra weeks to work on my technique. This new, longer preparation time would take the pressure off my weight loss attempt. I would be able to hit 67kg without the need to resort to extremes like running around Bangkok in a sweat suit.

The extra few weeks would also give me a chance to get my mind right for a fight; a chance to begin thinking a bit more like a fighter. I knew that mental training can make a huge difference when it comes to combat. I'd heard that experienced Nak Muay will spend a lot of time on mentally visualizing fights; imagining their opponent's moves and their reactions. That way the actual event will be less of a shock to the system. Some fighters mentally visualise every aspect of the encounter; trying to predict all the different scenarios that can occur with their opponent. Maybe this was something I could do even with busted ribs; although my lack of experience continued to make such visualisations difficult. I decided to devote more time to watching Muay Thai fights on TV; I could get to understand the action in these encounters a bit more this way.

Chapter 26

I CONTINUED TO TURN UP at Sitsongpeenong twice a day to train, but I waited two more weeks before trying to clinch or spar again. I now felt physically fit enough to last a few rounds in a Muay Thai fight. The only missing part of the jigsaw was sparring. My rib pain had settled down, but I still could not do sit-ups comfortably. Every day I'd turn down the offer to clinch; each time reminding the trainers that I had "jep sii krong" – sore ribs.

I became a bit paranoid. I suspected that some of the other Nak Muay saw my unwillingness to spar as malingering. This suspicion gained added weight when Marcus told me how he had entered a fight after taking a hard bang to his ribs on the eve of the confrontation. The moral of the story being that if I really wanted to fight I wouldn't let a few sore ribs get in the way; real men fight on regardless. This story put me in mind of the scene from the Monty Python film, *The Holy Grail*, where the knight keeps on attacking his foe even after his arms and legs have been cut off. You could say that this persistence in the face of injury makes people brave, but I see it as a bit reckless.

The problem with sore ribs is that there is no outward evidence for the injury; it is not like you get to wear a cast or anything. The fact that most of the time my ribs were pain-free meant that even I felt like a bit of a slacker sometimes. The discomfort only occurred when I touched the area or put pressure on it. I felt bad on every occasion that the trainer asked me to do something, and I had to turn them down. It meant breaking my earlier pledge to do exactly what they ordered. I kept on reminding myself not to worry what other people thought, but it did bother me. I just wanted my ribs to heal so that I could stop feeling like a malingerer.

I felt ready to give clinching another go. Khru Jack gave me an energetic thumbs-up when I confirmed that I would be taking part in Plam Muay that session. I even felt excited while taking my gloves and wraps off – not a hint of fear. A new group of foreigners had arrived at Sitsongpeenong that day and the trainer selected one of them as my opponent. We were about the same height and build. My opponent looked a bit nervous and this suited me fine. I felt eager to get down to business. I now knew that having to constantly say no to Plam Muay was harder to deal with than any slaps I might pick up inside the ring.

The clinching session lasted less than a minute. My opponent just tapped me once in the ribs and I had to stop. He didn't hit me hard, but it felt like being slapped with a sledgehammer. My ribs were nowhere near as healed as I'd hoped. The other guy noticed me wince and asked if everything was OK. I wanted to continue, but a couple of seconds later he touched the same area again, and I had to pull away. I could not continue. I felt a huge sense of disappointment as the implications of this hit home. I climbed back out of the ring.

I felt annoyed when Khru Jack asked me why I didn't want to clinch – wasn't it obvious? I smiled and gave my standard reply of, "jep sii krong" – knowing that I must sound like a broken record. We were joined by Nut; the woman who took care of the administration side of things at Sitsongpeenong. She also wanted to know why I'd quit clinching after just a couple of seconds. I explained to her all about the jeb sii krong. She asked why I had not gone to the hospital to have things checked out. I could no longer think of a good answer to this.

The idea of going to a doctor now made sense. I'd put it off because I didn't think there was much that they could do for me. I felt desperate now; at least they would be able to tell me if my ribs were broken or bruised. Perhaps they could offer some drug that would drastically speed up the healing process – it needed to be good because I wanted to be able to clinch and spar right away. This really was clutching at straws, but it delayed having to face the inevitable. My time working as a nurse meant that deep down I knew that expectations of a secret rib healing treatment for desperate middle-aged Muay Thai fighters were a bit unrealistic.

I took my wife and son with me to the local private hospital in Minburi. I knew that if I went to the Government hospital it could take all day so I didn't mind paying a bit of money to speed things along. My plan was to go to the hospital, get my ribs fixed, and be able to clinch by the afternoon session. I felt like a man on death row who had one last chance of escaping the sentence; I desperately wanted to believe in this last chance even though it was probably hopeless. Maybe this mysterious force that had been pushing me toward this fight would pull a magic rabbit out of the hat now. It is possible to convince yourself of anything if you are desperate enough.

I didn't have to wait long before a nurse came along to shepherd me into a treatment room; this speediness reassured me that I had made the right choice by going private. My self-congratulations ended when I entered the room. The doctor waited within with his head on the desk. I hoped that this just meant that he was tired and not having some type of nervous breakdown. The nurse showed no signs of nervousness so I guessed this confirmed tiredness rather than insanity. I've seen the long hours that doctors put in, but I couldn't help feeling that this guy was taking the piss. When I go private I've got high hopes and part of this is a doctor who at least looks alert when I arrive in his office.

My entry disturbed the physician. When he lifted his head up from the desk he made an audible groan. He probably thought that he was now going to have to deal with a foreigner who couldn't speak Thai. Doctors in Thailand all learn English during their training but many of them don't like to speak it. I can understand this. He looked a bit less despondent when I explained the situation as best as I could in Thai. His look of concern about having to speak English turned to lack of interest as I explained my situation. I'd started off on my petition for how I needed some medicine that would help me be ready for clinching right away when he cut me short – he wanted me to go get an x-ray.

I was taken for the x-ray without any waiting – great service. I felt a bit surprised when the radiologist only took one picture of my left side. I tried to explain that the jep sii krong was a little bit to the front of my chest, but he answered briskly that this wouldn't be a problem; if there was any damage they would see it on the side view x-ray. There didn't seem to be any point in further questions. I just needed to have faith that these people knew what they were doing. It wasn't like rib pain would be considered a rare condition or anything.

Once the x-ray had been processed I was taken back to see the doctor. This time he sat upright when I entered his office. He had my x-ray on the lighting board behind him. He pointed vaguely in that direction and told me that he couldn't see any broken ribs. This meant that they were probably bruised. He closed my folder as if ready to dismiss me. I went back into my speech about how I needed to be ready for Muay Thai sparring that afternoon and asked him how this could be accomplished. He seemed unable to understand my predicament his only response was to give me a disapproving look and say that Muay Thai is dangerous.

The physician went on to say that he would write me up for a few painkillers. This did not thrill me at all because I knew that in Thailand you always got sent home with painkillers no matter what problem you came in with. He must have noticed my disappointment because his face suddenly lit up as if he had a great idea. He would be able to give me a hydrocortisone injection and this would help with the inflammation. I appreciated this idea and agreed to it. Deep down though, I knew that at best such an injection would only provide a short-term reduction in pain. I would have refused it if I'd known that I would have to wait another two hours before the nurses got around to giving me this injection. This meant that the temporary easing of symptoms seemed unnecessary because it was already too late to go to the afternoon training session anyway.

I could now no longer deny the obvious. I would not be able to fight even with the additional three weeks. If I continued to train full-time it would just mean spending more money – something that I couldn't afford to do. The only sensible thing was to go back to part-time training right away. The idea of this left me feeling incredibly sad. It meant giving up on my dream, but it didn't feel like I had any choice in the matter. I could not justify training full-time any longer unless there was a good chance that I would get to fight – there was now no chance of this.

As well as a sense of sadness and regret I must admit that I also experienced a slight sense of relief. I'd spent so much time worrying about fighting without adequate preparation. It kept me awake at night. I had regular nightmares of being beaten to a pulp inside the ring, and I'd carry these fears around with me for the rest of the day. My couple of experiences with sparring only emphasised my lack of preparedness to fight Muay Thai. Even this slight sense of relief came packed with a good dollop of guilt – why should I feel relieved to be losing out on a dream?

Chapter 27

I DIDN'T GO TO SITSONGPEENONG at all for the next two days. It felt like bunking off from school. I could have finished off the rest of the week full-time but decided to just mope around at home instead. I suspected that this had been my one and only chance to fight Muay Thai, and I'd just lost it. I knew that I'd probably never be able to devote myself to training like that again. It sort of felt like I'd just had this amazing romantic fling, but now I'd been dumped.

I felt sorry for myself and even considered giving up Muay Thai altogether. I could no longer see the point of going to Sitsongpeenong just to train if it wasn't going to lead to a fight. I suspected that the trainers would lose interest in me once they knew that I wasn't planning to step into the ring anytime soon. I would just be somebody who turns up for a bit of exercise. I might as well just join a local aerobics class.

I'd already cleared my diary to make room for full-time training so I now had a bit of free time on my hands until I could get things rolling again. I spent most of it on the internet. I kept reading blogs written by people who trained Muay Thai. I'd no idea what I was hoping to find, but just felt driven to keep looking. At times it felt like I was just trying to punish myself; a morbid reminder of what I had just given up. I felt heartbroken. I acted like one of those people who hide in their bedroom and listen to love songs after they've been dumped by their partner. It took quite a bit of time wallowing online before the obvious finally hit me. There were many people who were able to fight Muay Thai yet still hold down full-time jobs.

I'd spent a bit of time whining on one of the online Muay Thai forums about my ribs. I now asked the members on there about their opinions as to the need to train full-time in order to fight. The overall opinion was that you did not necessarily have to be training full-time. In fact a couple of guys gave convincing arguments for why it might be better not to train full-time. They reckoned that it was just overkill and that too many people over-trained and picked up injuries as a result. These ideas made a lot of sense to me. It also gave me great hope; maybe I could still fight Muay Thai after all.

If I worked hard to keep up my cardiovascular fitness and went to Sitsongpeenong three or four times a week then there would be no real reason why I wouldn't be able to fight in a few more months. This would give me plenty of time for my ribs to recover, and do the necessary preparations for fighting. It would take a lot of pressure off me. Just as I was about to give up on my goal another door had opened which would allow me to achieve it.

I felt a bit sheepish returning to the gym but nobody asked me why I hadn't been training for the last few days. Why would they? People come and go all the time at Sitsongpeenong, and it wasn't like I was their star fighter or anything. To me it felt like I'd been away for ages, but it had only been a couple of days. It felt good to be back with my new and more realistic goal. I shared my ideas about fighting while training part-time with a few people; they all agreed that it sounded like a good plan.

I got talking to one of the new arrivals at Sitsongpeenong; an Australian guy called Mike who was in his late thirties. He shared a story that gave me even more reason to feel hopeful. He had gotten into the ring the first time with hardly any sparring experience. He just kept his cool and managed to do fairly well. In fact he only lost the fight because of a decision. This was inspiring stuff for me. I could see that ideally it would be best to get as much sparring experience as possible but maybe it wasn't as vital as I'd been thinking. Perhaps if I just got a bit more comfortable with sparring I'd be safe enough for my first fight.

One of the big difficulties with going back to part-time training would be maintaining my current fitness level. The idea of just running around the outside of the house again no longer seemed like an effective solution. I enjoyed running in Suan Luang, but it was just too far away for me to make that journey every day. I got out the map but couldn't see a park that was any nearer to my home. I was moaning to my wife when she suggested running in the local stadium. It seemed like a great idea to me, and I asked Oa why she had never suggested it before. Apparently she had, but I hadn't been listening.

The stadium was only a couple of kilometres away; I'd be able to get there in a few minutes on my motorbike. I went along with Oa to check it out, and they said that I could run outside the stadium for free or become a member and run inside on the track. The price of the yearly membership was just 20 baht (less than half a euro) so signing up felt like the obvious choice. I would now have my own place to run each day, and there would be no need to drive Oa, or my neighbours, crazy by running around the outside of the house.

The other nice thing about training part-time was that maybe if I liked fighting it could be something that I could do on a regular basis. Who knows, perhaps I could have some type of fighting career right in the middle of my forties. I'd heard about one woman who had done just that and afterwards became a Muay Thai trainer. Of course the only real drawback about my plan is that I'd so far shown no real inclination towards fighting. It had now become something that I just wanted to get done so that I could check the goal off my list of ambitions.

I had heard that there were reluctant fighters who fell in love with fighting after they got the first one out of the way. Apparently there is nothing else like stepping into the ring to fight; sparring does not even come close. The only way that you can find out if you like it is by actually doing it. Who knows, maybe I could step into the ring and turn into some type of tiger – it's nice to dream. So perhaps it wasn't such a huge leap in imagination to think that I might fight more than once.

One of the things I'd noticed about a lot of the foreigners who train at Sitsongpeenong is that they love to watch other people fight. At the end of their training session they will often gather round and spend some time watching the Thai fighters. Kem Sitsongpeenong would usually attract a crowd of wide-eyed admirers when he clinched. I'm sure they learn a lot from observing such skilled Nak Muay, but it is also obvious that they do it because they like it. One thing that worries me about Muay Thai is that I've usually no real urge to watch other people fight – or at least not enough to stay on at the gym after the session has ended.

I loved the training most of the time but worried that my lack of passion for watching the sport might be a bad omen. Maybe this accounted for my failure to progress as a fighter in the way I would have liked. I just did not want it enough. I'd heard about guys who continued to spar even though they had busted ribs and other injuries. I admired their determination, but I just did not have that same drive.

I remember how Marcus had told me that he spent a lot of his free time researching techniques and practicing things over and over again in front of the mirror. He really delved into the science behind everything, and I admired him greatly for this. When I was younger I had a similar attitude. I loved Kung Fu, and thinking about it all the time required no effort – it was what I did all the time anyway. Now though, there were just too many things going on in my life, and maybe this was a huge part of the problem.

Maybe if I wasn't struggling to make a living and didn't have a wife and kid I would be happy to stay for hours at Sitsongpeenong to watch other people spar. Who knows? The one thing I do know is that this was not something that appealed to me now. I just wanted to train and go home at the end of the session.

Chapter 28

THE MOMENTUM FROM THE FULL-TIME training meant that exercising for a couple of hours each day at home didn't feel like much of a challenge. The decision to run in the local stadium worked out well. I would get there about 5.30am in the morning and try to run for an hour. I would have the track to myself for the first few minutes but by 6.30am it would be quite busy. I enjoyed the atmosphere inside the stadium; it had a real community feel to it. People would say hello when we passed each other; occasionally somebody would fall into step with me and we would chat in Thai or English for a few laps.

Most of those who turned up at the stadium seemed to only train a couple of times a week. This meant that I was usually the fastest guy on the track and nobody else ran for the same duration as me; most people gave up after about 20 minutes. I had the rare feeling of being better at something than most other people around me. Considering my recent performance at Sitsongpeenong it felt nice; even though I knew my self-assurance in my newfound running abilities bordered on the verge of arrogance. Occasionally some of the more competitive runners would whiz past me, but they would usually run out of steam after a couple of laps and give up. The only exception to this was one man who appeared to be about the same age as me. He looked to be a very experienced runner and he would pass me about every fifth lap. He never ran for longer than 30 minutes.

I had to keep reminding myself to take it easy because the aim was to keep up my fitness and not to be racing and trying to show off. I worried that if I pushed myself too hard I'd pick up another injury. I'd had problems with my knees in the past and worried that there would be a recurrence. I did still get the occasional twinge in my knee after a long workout. If I wasn't able to run then this would make it almost impossible to keep my fitness level up. It was just so hard not to race when going around a track with other people; the sense of competition made it more exciting and most important of all it made the time go faster.

Some of the people who turned up to exercise at Minburi stadium were real characters. One of my favourites was a woman who looked to be in her seventies. She would walk around the track waving a hanky in the air; wriggling her hips as she walked. Sometimes her movements appeared quite sexy in a disturbing way; maybe I was turning into some type of pervert. It all looked a bit strange but this fitness regime worked for her because she seemed so physically fit. If I reached her age and was still able to keep going like that I'd be very happy. Part of her routine was running up and down the stands at the side of the track; something that I would have struggled to do. The idea of copying her routine didn't appeal to me at all despite its apparent effectiveness – I just don't have the hips for it.

As well as the adults there were also lots of school

kids using the track too. One morning I got to speak with one of their teachers; he fell in beside me as I was running. He told me that these kids went to a special school where the focus was on athletics. Some of these youngsters would go on to represent Thailand in international sporting events. They all looked very dedicated and full of youthful enthusiasm. I had felt that sort of devotion towards martial arts at their age, but unfortunately I didn't possess the same natural talent as these kids. I couldn't imagine any of these fresh faced youngsters falling into addiction. The teacher assured me that they were the cream of the crop in Thailand.

I liked to finish my run just as the young athletes arrived on the track. There were quite a few of them so they could take up quite a lot of space. They would congregate at one end of the track and getting past them while running could be like going through an obstacle course. I didn't like getting in their way because they should have priority over fun-runners like me. I also felt slightly irritated when they would all whiz past me; it ruined my illusion of being the fitness king at Minburi stadium. So I did try to arrange it so that my final victory lap each day would take place while they were still warming up.

One morning I was joined by a Minburi regular. I'd noticed him a few times but we had never spoken before this. He had an unusual look for a Thai; completely bald with a goatee. He kept pace with me for the last 30 minutes of my run. I felt a bit shocked when he admitted to being in his late sixties – I never would have guessed. He claimed cycling as his main passion, but he still managed to run three or four mornings a week. I admired him for his fitness level and joie de vivre.

My running partner was giving my Thai language skills a good workout. My comprehension level for Thai is fairly fluent, but sometimes I struggle when putting a sentence together. I suppose it is a type of laziness, but it is also to do with the fact that sometimes I just do not like to talk too much – even in English. There are days when you can't shut me up, but at other times I just prefer to be quiet. His list of questions seemed never ending, but I replied to each one as best as I could.

As we would pass people on the run my new pal would share titbits of the information I'd just given him. It felt a bit embarrassing to hear him tell everyone we passed my age and nationality. I made the mistake of telling him that I was training at Muay Thai. He began telling everyone that I was this big Muay Thai star from Europe. I had to do a lot of backtracking to convince him that when it came to Muay Thai I was definitely at novice level. He accepted my explanation, but he made no attempt to clarify the situation with the other people on the track. They still probably have this idea that I'm some type of professional fighter. Thankfully nobody has challenged me to combat in order to test my skills.

My new friend seemed disappointed when I told him that this would be my last lap of the day. He still had plenty of energy left, and he showed no sign of running out of questions. He was a nice old guy, but I sincerely hoped that he wouldn't be joining me every day. He could have made a fortune as an interrogator. As I left the stadium I couldn't help worrying that I'd given him way too much information about myself. What if he was some type of scam artist? He surely had enough information about me now to convincingly steal my identity.

For the next few runs I was joined by other people. The companionship and chat did make the time pass more quickly, but I sort of missed running alone. While training full-time my meditation practice had hit a wall; it still had not recovered. I just wasn't able to sit down and meditate any more. It felt like I had too much energy and it couldn't be confined in the lotus position. I've known for a long time that you do not need to sit cross-legged in order to meditate; it is possible to do it while engaging in practically any activity so long as you have sufficient concentration. I'd hoped to make up for my lack of formal meditation practice by meditating as I ran. This had worked for my first few runs, but just couldn't be done while running with a crowd.

I decided that the best solution would be to arrive at the track earlier in the morning. It was always deserted for the first few minutes of my run, so if I came 30 minutes earlier that would give me sufficient solo time. I could still be able to run in the company of others for the last few minutes. This would also mean that I'd be less tempted to overdo things as there would be nobody to compete against for most of the run. It made a lot of sense even if it did suggest that I was a bit of an unsociable character.

One of the other nice benefits of coming earlier was that it meant that I would be running on the track as the world woke up. The view of the sunrise wasn't great because the stadium stands blocked most of the view. I would only catch glimpses of the sun as I hit the corner parts of the stadium where there was no seating. Still it was nice to just be there at that time of the day. When I'd start my run the track would be in darkness; the only lighting would come from a few streetlights outside. I would noticeably observe that the day was getting brighter with each passing lap; by around my tenth loop of the track it would be fully light and other people would start arriving.

The stadium is right in the path of Suvarnabhumi Airport so planes constantly fly overhead. I tried to see if there was ever a time when the sky above didn't have a visible plane and it never happened. It felt so nice running while these planes passed overhead. I kept thinking of all those excited people who were just about to land in Thailand. It brought up memories of when I first arrived. There is also something about airplanes that really excites me; I never get bored of them. The only problem is that it gives me itchy feet to go travelling again; something that is no longer practical now that I have a wife and son.

The morning runs were keeping my cardiovascular fitness at a nice level. I made it to Sitsongpeenong three times a week, and I trained every afternoon at home. I could see that I wasn't going to be as fit as during my time training twice a day at Sitsongpeenong, but I'd be close to it. I would probably only need to increase the intensity of my training a couple of weeks before any fight and that would be enough to get me ready.

Chapter 29

WE WERE NOW IN LATE July. It seemed that every time I turned up at Sitsongpeenong there were more people training. One afternoon there were so many people that it was difficult to get any time with a trainer. I asked Tim about it and he said that it was due to it being the summer holidays in Europe and the US. A lot of people were using this time to get some intense training in Thailand. I couldn't blame them, but I selfishly resented the fact that the gym was now so overrun with people.

Tim responded to the increased number of students by putting the afternoon class back to 2pm. It meant that the foreigners would begin training an hour before the Thai fighters. This development alarmed me because there was no way I'd be able to make it that early. I had to pick up my son from school at 2pm so the earliest I could make the gym would be 2.45pm. I told Tim about my concerns, and he agreed to let me keep coming at 3pm. Arriving an hour late to class meant that I was starting when all the other foreigners were winding down. The Thai students did their own thing, and they were too far above my level for me to join in with them.

My late arrival put me at a great disadvantage when it came to training. The trainers would have already held pads for three or four people by the time they got to me. This meant that they were already exhausted, and so this tended to mean a half-hearted effort. I was back training with Khru Jack most of the time, and he was doing little more than going through the motions. I could see that these trainers now had a lot of extra work, but it just made the session seem a bit pointless for me. During one pad session Khru Jack kept walking off to talk to people; he didn't do this once but many times. I couldn't even work up a sweat.

I still wasn't able to clinch and spar so the only real purpose for coming to the gym was pad work. I could punch a bag at home. So if I couldn't get a good workout with a trainer the trip was just a waste of my time; two hours sitting in traffic jams for nothing. I kept on returning to Sitsongpeenong anyway. I knew that things would quieten down in a few weeks, and I just hoped that Tim would go back to the 3 pm start. Another problem with the earlier start was that I would be doing pads when everyone else would be clinching and sparring. This meant that even when my ribs had healed I'd still be struggling to get some fighting experience.

My plan had been to continue staying at the gym for a two hour training session. In reality though I rarely stayed more than an hour and a half these days; once the other foreigners had left there seemed to be little point in staying. The trainers had all their focus on the Thai fighters, and I would get bored kicking the bags alone. I would do a bit of weight training, but I didn't really know how to use them properly. I'd picked up a couple of exercises from watching the others, but my technique with the weights wasn't great.

I had hit a plateau in my training. There seemed to

be no further progress to be made until my ribs healed and I could return to sparring; instead I just worked hard to keep still. I felt frustrated to be training all the time without any sign of a fight on the horizon, and no more evidence of improvement in my skills. I wondered how long I could keep it up.

I considered looking for a new Muay Thai gym in the hope that a fresh approach might help. I'd heard a lot of people say that Sitsongpeenong is about the best gym in Bangkok, but I had nothing to compare it with. I sometimes wondered if it was more suited to the younger more experienced fighter. Most of the foreigners who turned up at the gym all had the basics mastered and so there was no real focus on this at Sitsongpeenong. I didn't feel like I had even covered the basic elements of technique yet. I wondered if I might do better if I changed gym.

I spent a whole afternoon searching the web for alternative Muay Thai gym options in Bangkok. There were plenty of them to choose from but most of them were too far away from Minburi. I already found the journey to be a real hassle so choosing a gym further that would involve more travelling didn't seem like an attractive option to me.

In the end I decided to just stay at Sitsongpeenong. I'd already come this far with them and it felt like home. I also realised that all the good gyms were going to be busy at this time of year just like Sitsongpeenong. I consoled myself with the knowledge that things would quieten down at the camp again soon and I'd get more time with the trainers.

Chapter 30

IT TOOK SIX WEEKS BEFORE my ribs healed enough for me to be able to return to clinching and sparring. We had now entered August and Sitsongpeenong had reached full-capacity; it was hard to do anything without bumping into somebody. I didn't really get to know this new cohort of foreigners because of my usual late arrival at the gym. There were a couple of guys over from England, and I made a point of talking to them. Both of these men were older than me and neither of them had any intention of fighting in the future. They just liked the training. I sort of envied them their no-pressure attitude to Muay Thai. I wanted to return to that frame of mind once I got the fight out of the way.

I now felt ready to spar but didn't know how this would be possible. All the foreigners tended to be gone from the gym by the time I'd finished on the pads. I mentioned this to Khru Jack. He suggested that I skip the warm up and just hop in the ring as soon as I arrived in the afternoon. The idea of sparring without any warm up seemed a bit strange, but I couldn't think of a better option. I arranged to pick up my son from school a few minutes earlier and this meant that I could now reach Sitsongpeenong by 2.30pm. Because of how busy it had become at the camp there would already be people sparring at 2.30pm and I could join them. I would put on my hand wraps as soon as I arrived and hop in the ring to fight.

The crowd problem at Sitsongpeenong also meant that the rules of sparring had changed; we were only allowed to box and not to kick. I guess that this meant that more people could be sparring inside the ring at the one time; it also made it easier for the trainers to control things. My last attempt to get back in the ring after the rib injury had been short-lived but this time there would be no stopping me. I felt excited. Almost as if returning to a much loved activity that had been denied me; a strange way for me to be thinking considering how much I hated sparring before. I suppose that the continuous setbacks were just pissing me off so much that I wanted to just get in there. I also felt more confident because Marcus no longer trained at Sitsongpeenong; he just disappeared one day without a word. The fact that he would no longer be around to knock the shit out of me removed some of my reservations about fighting. I doubted there would be anyone else who would be as tough an opponent when sparring – maybe he really had done me a great favour after all.

The foreign students had already started sparring by the time I arrived for my return to the ring. This meant that I only got to join them for the final two rounds. This suited me perfectly because it would mean an easier introduction. My first opponent was a young Vietnamese American. I had a slight advantage in height but we looked to be about the same weight. I'd seen him a couple of times before, but I had no real idea about his capabilities as a fighter. I did know that he had a fight coming up. He almost definitely had a lot more skill and experience than I did, but this knowledge didn't leave me feeling intimidated. If I could at least put in a good effort then I would be satisfied no matter how well he performed.

We started sparring and I surprised myself by landing a few punches on him. He hit me more than I hit him, but his punches were nowhere near as hard as Marcus' had been. Initially he seemed confident enough to just land a few punches every time I opened my guard to attack him. When he did this the first couple of times it did cause a bit of panic, but once I realised that his strikes weren't going to do that much damage I became more daring. I caught him with a couple of nice jabs and could feel him backing off. That was such a great feeling for me. I just kept on attacking him; delighted to find that so many of my punches were actually landing. I could hear Khru Jack in the background saying "good, good".

My opponent appeared to lose some of his confidence. He could see that I wasn't very good yet he wasn't able to keep on top of me. He started coming after me a bit harder, but this made him clumsier. I wasn't scared of him now at all and I kept on landing punches. Some of my strikes hit him at odd angles and didn't have any power, but he didn't like the fact that I kept on getting past his guard. My first sparring sessions had all gone by in a horrible blur, but now I experienced a sense of clarity. I could see the gaping holes in my opponent's defences so I could now take advantage of them. There were a few times when I went on the attack that I actually saw fear in his eyes.

I felt encouraged when my next opponent appeared hesitant and nervous. To start the round he sent a couple of half-hearted punches in my direction but they were easy to evade. I began working on my jab and found that this put him completely on the defensive. After a few of my punches made contact he just hid with his arms up around his head; exactly like I'd done when fighting Marcus. For the first time in a fight against another person I felt in almost total control. I could now hit the many holes in his defences at will. I remembered how Marcus had battered me with his hooks when I'd been hidden behind my hands. I tried a few hooks but they turned out to be terribly ineffective. They had no power in them at all; my technique was horrible. I returned to just a combination of jabs and punches.

My opponent no longer seemed capable of defending himself, and I started to feel like a bit of a bully. I stopped to ask him if he felt alright to continue, and he said that he was fine. I couldn't just continue slapping him hard though if he wasn't going to put up a fight. I remembered how bad I'd felt when Marcus had done that to me. So for the last minute I just powered down and would only throw out the occasional jab and punch combination. My opponent reacted to my decrease in intensity by offering an occasional punch as well. He remained nervous of my strikes, and I always seemed to be pressing forward.

After the fight I went back to the punch bags to wait for my turn on the pads with Khru Jack. The Vietnamese American chap, who had been my first opponent that day, came over to talk to me. He started pointing out all the things I'd done wrong while sparring against him. I had become used to the other students at the gym giving me advice, and I usually felt grateful for it but not so much this time. This guy just irritated me because I could see that his real motive here was to save face; it wasn't like he had been particularly impressive himself. Many of the things he mentioned could have been equally said about his own performance. He did point out that I wasn't fully committing myself to the punches, and I agreed with him on that. On a positive note he did say that I'd been a tough opponent who had shown no fear; the complete opposite to how I felt up until this point. I still didn't appreciate his attempt to lecture me though.

I actually felt a bit elated by my performance. I'd gone up against two guys and hadn't made a clown of myself. In fact if it had been a competition I would have almost certainly won against the second opponent. This to me was a huge improvement on how I usually felt at Sitsongpeenong. There were even moments when I'd enjoyed sparring that day –something that I would not have believed possible before. Maybe I really could grow to like fighting after all.

My satisfaction with the sparring was also tinged with a tiny bit of unease. I had seen a look of fear in my opponent's eye and I liked it. This unease increased when I found out that my second opponent had been a lot younger than he looked. I heard him tell one of the other guys that he was only 17. I was well over twice his age and I'd just been smacking him around the head. He seemed like a gentle sort of kid. Apparently he had travelled to Thailand alone so that he could train; I deeply admired his courage and determination. At 17 I'd already started drinking heavily and the process of flushing my life down the toilet had been well under way. I would have liked to have gone up and asked him how he was doing; that would have given me a bit of reassurance that there were no hard feelings. He was in deep conversation with a group of other new arrivals. I left the camp feeling a bit elated and a bit guilty at the same time in case I might be turning into a psychopath who enjoyed inflicting pain on people.

I made it even earlier to the next session at Sitsongpeenong and this time I was able to make it through four rounds of sparring. I felt confident getting into the ring. I ended up doing two rounds with my first opponent. We did go to change partner at the end of round one, but everyone had already been paired up so we were left facing each other again. I didn't mind. This guy had a lot of skill but he didn't seem to have any urge to dominate me. On a couple of occasions he even stopped to show me how I could improve my technique.

At the end of the third round I got paired up against a Belgian guy. He was tall and strong, and had a tranquil look on his face that I found a bit unsettling. His calm features turned out to be a ruse because right away he landed a flurry of hard punches to my head. I could feel my brain buzzing, but for some reason I wasn't so put off by this anymore. I just kept on coming back at him. Every time he would hit me I would just go after him. I could see by his expression that some of the punches hurt him. He retaliated with harder and longer flurries of punches, but I kept on answering this with more intensive attacks of my own. Somewhere in the back of my mind was the vague worry that these punches to my head couldn't be doing me much good, but I didn't care. I realised that the worst thing was the fear of the punches not the punches themselves.

Despite the intensity of the sparring I'd totally enjoyed it. If the trainer had said for us to go another round I would have agreed. For a few minutes my whole world had been in that ring; there had just been me and this other guy struggling to gain dominance – nothing else had seemed important. Maybe this was why people really liked to fight so much. This is the type of focus I strive for in meditation yet here it had happened spontaneously. For those few minutes while fighting my mind had been completely in the moment, and it had felt wonderful. It hadn't been about anger or violence. It had felt like I'd shared something special with my opponent.

I felt on a high when I faced my next opponent – a red headed German. He looked a bit dazed, and after I sent a couple of jabs in his direction I could tell that something was not right. I asked him what was wrong and he explained that he'd just been hit in the head really hard and had not yet recovered from the effects of the blow. He said he'd be fine in a minute. We began sparring again, but it was obvious that this guy needed to stop – his pupils looked like saucers. I called one of the trainers over, and he escorted my opponent out of the ring. The Belgian guy congratulated me on an impressive technical knockout. There was nobody left for me to fight, but I just stayed in the ring to watch the other fighters. For the first time at Sitsongpeenong it felt like I really belonged in the ring.

Chapter 31

OVER THE NEXT FEW WEEKS the intensity of my training began to decrease. I had plenty of justifications for this. Some days I would just have too many work commitments to be able to exercise twice a day. We were now in the rainy season so this would give me an excuse to miss runs. I now only managed to make it to Minburi stadium every second day. Instead of getting to the gym four times a week I struggled to go more than twice a week. I had no sense of urgency to be in top physical condition and this made it easier to do less.

I still felt in great shape physically. It would only take me two or three weeks to get back to the level of fitness I would need to be ready to fight. I didn't see the point in overdoing things until then. I'd brought my weight down to 67kg, and maintaining this felt easy. I'd gotten used to the diet, and it didn't feel like too much of an effort. I actually enjoyed eating every three hours because it gave me an excuse to take regular breaks from the computer. So once I had a date for a fight the only real work would be to increase my fitness again. I already knew that I had the ability to reach that level of physical conditioning.

I would spar at almost every session and no longer felt on the verge of a panic attack when asked to put on the big gloves. I'd been picking up a lot of facial bruises from the boxing, but these didn't bother me so much. I saw it as all just part of the training – Muay Thai isn't ballet after all. I still had a lot of work to do, but the idea of actually one day stepping into a ring no longer seemed like such a big deal.

When Khru Jack asked if I wanted to fight it took me by surprise. This turned to shock when he explained that the encounter was only a week away; apparently another fighter had pulled out at the last minute. I felt chuffed that he would consider me ready to fight, but there was also the undeniable feeling in my gut that one week would not be long enough to prepare. He explained that the event was still only a possibility, and that he could not give me any information about who I'd be up against. All he could say was that it was going to be at MBK department store. I told him to find out more about the fight, and I'd consider it. I couldn't concentrate for the rest of the session because my mind went into shock at the possibility of an actual fight so soon.

Before going home that day I managed to corner Tim. He didn't seem to have much more information than Khru Jack about what the fight would involve. He also seemed even less sure about it actually taking place. I mentioned my concerns about not being prepared. He said not to worry about this fight if I wasn't ready, because there should be a lot more fights coming up. Apparently Sitsongpeenong had arranged this new deal with a fighting venue in Pattaya, and they would have something suitable for someone like me over the coming months.

The suggestion of a fight at some indefinite time in the future felt a lot more appealing to me than a fight the following Saturday. It gave me the perfect alibi for ducking out of this more imminent opportunity. It would mean that I could say no to Khru Jack without feeling like a coward; I was just being sensible is all. I grabbed onto Tim's suggestion as if it were a life raft.

I was told about this fight on a Friday afternoon, and I promised to think about it over the weekend. Deep down I had already made my mind up, but I told myself that I would give it serious consideration. I even mentioned the possibility of the fight to Oa. She looked worried, but could see that a fight at MBK might be an exciting evening out. After all, MBK is situated in Siam Square where all the most fashionable shops in Bangkok can be found. I told Oa about the other alternative to fight at a later date in Pattaya. I felt a bit disappointed when she didn't insist that this would be a better idea. I could tell that Oa continued to view my desire to fight as a bit reckless, but she had grown to accept it.

I didn't train much over that weekend. I woke up too late on the Saturday to do my morning run. On Sunday I just wanted to get out of the house so I took Oa and Timmy away for the day. This meant that if I did decide to take this fight I'd have four days to train for it – I'd be expected to rest on the eve of the encounter. The idea of having so little time to prepare for the fight just seemed ludicrous. It offered the final excuse, I needed to say no.

I had this eager anticipation to get into Sitsongpeenong on that Monday. Not because I wanted to train but because I wanted to let them know about my decision not to fight. I knew that they would need my agreement in order to schedule it, but I had this irrational worry that unless I gave them a clear no they would sign me up for it anyway.

Khru Jack looked a bit disappointed with me when I told him that I didn't want to fight. I'd cornered him almost the minute I got through the door of the gym. I gave him the top five of my excuses, but he didn't seem impressed with any of them. It was obvious that he just saw me as one of those guys who didn't want to get into the ring. I'd always have an excuse not to fight – I couldn't help but suspect that he was right.

I got hold of Tim and explained my decision to him. He didn't look at all surprised because it was probably obvious to him from our last encounter that I wasn't that keen. I told him that I would definitely take the next fight that came along. He said "sure", but he no longer looked convinced of my willingness to fight either.

Chapter 32

By mid August the mood in the gym had become serious. The reason for this tension was that five of the foreigners were going to be fighting soon. It would be their first, and probably only, fight in Thailand for most of them. As far as I could tell they all had amateur fights back in their home countries, but fighting in Thailand was going to be a whole new ballgame. I could now see how much guts it took to take on a fight; I envied them their bravery. I tried to console myself with the idea that all these guys were a lot more experienced than me, but deep down I knew that they had a determination that I just did not possess – at least at the moment anyway.

The intensity of the sparring had increased as people got nearer to their fights. The blows were noticeably harder and nobody was taking it easy during sparring. Even the people who weren't due to fight were becoming caught up in the atmosphere of the gym and picking up their game. The fact that Sitsongpeenong continued to be so crowded only added to the intensely serious mood at the camp.

I now often felt like I'd no fear during sparring sessions. I'd completely gotten over my terror of being hit, and moved to the other extreme of just ignoring other people's attacks. I now almost liked absorbing blows with my face. I would get hammered, but I was also managing to get a lot of hits on other people. I would go home and look at my facial bruises and feel a bit proud of them. I saw them as a sign of my status as a Muay Thai fighter. It reminded me of how the guys in the movie *Fight Club* had felt proud of their bruises too.

For the first time in my life I felt like a warrior. I didn't even consider the possibility that I shouldn't be picking up so much damage. I failed to notice that most of the other people I fought with would walk away from the sparring session with hardly a mark on them. I had become too caught up in my amazement of being able to take a punch.

It turned out to be social embarrassment that finally convinced me that my new found bravery wasn't such a good thing. It was coming up to Mother's Day in Thailand, and my son was due to give a performance at his local school. My wife and I were invited to attend. We were excited because this would be his first time doing anything like this. Oa had expressed concerns about the number of bruises I'd been picking up recently. I waved her concerns off by pointing out that I was training at Muay Thai not ballet dancing – bruises were just part of it. She didn't appear convinced by my logic.

It was three days before Mother's Day when the novelty of being hit began to wear off. At this particular session at Sitsongpeenong I had managed to soak up a ridiculous number of hits. I didn't seem to be getting punched harder than any other day, but the number of absorbed blows insured that by the end of the session my face looked the worst for wear.

A couple of people in the gym had expressed concern, but it wasn't until I got home though, that I realised how much damage had been done. Both sides of my face were black and blue. It looked terrible, and I felt so guilty when I noticed how concerned Timmy looked. Oa was not one bit happy, but I tried to reassure her that everything would be fine by Mother's Day. Once again my overly optimistic expectations of my healing capacity was giving me false comfort. I promised to not go training again until after our son's performance, but this really was shutting the stable door after the horse had fucked off.

Of course my face was still a mess by Mother's Day. I reluctantly tried my wife's makeup to cover up the worst of the bruising, but the foundation made little difference. I felt too embarrassed by my appearance to go to the event, and I felt terribly guilty about this. It was going to be an important day for my son, but I would not be there. Oa did her best to hide her annoyance, and she promised to record the event on my video camera – so at least I wouldn't fully miss out on Timmy's debut on the stage.

Oa left with Timmy to go to his show. I tried to concentrate on work, but I continued to feel bad about missing his performance. In the end I got into my car and went to his school. I need not have bothered because by the time I arrived he had already been up on the stage. I could feel every eye on me and my bruised face. My son's English teacher came over to say hello, and I automatically went into a big discussion about my bruises. I blathered on like I had something to hide and wanted to cover up my shame. He probably thought that in reality I'd fallen down drunk somewhere. I couldn't blame him for thinking this way because I was acting guilty as hell. In the end I had to settle for a video of my son performing his song – 'Mama, I Love You' by the Spice Girls. He did an excellent job, and I really felt proud of him.

This experience convinced me that getting hit all the time wasn't such a good thing. It was nice to know that I could take a punch, but now I would need to concentrate on avoiding them a bit more. If I didn't then I would probably end up with a lot more damage than just facial bruising. I would stop viewing bruises as an emblem of pride and instead see them for what they are – evidence that I needed to defend a lot better.

Chapter 33

I MADE UP MY MIND to avoid being a punching bag at my next sparring session. From now on I would concentrate more on defending myself. The only problem with this was that I didn't really know how to do that. We didn't spend too much time at the camp learning defensive techniques. Only rarely did the trainers make suggestions for how I could avoid being hit by using blocks. The only exception to this would be the block against the turning kick where I would bring my knee up; I would get to practice that technique each session. I had no real idea how to block or evade punches or front kicks.

The only other defensive technique that I practiced fairly regularly would be putting my arms up around my head and hoping for the best. I hesitate to call this a defensive technique because it felt more like trying to weather the storm. I'd still feel a lot of the blows. Khru Jack liked to practise this one with me a lot. During pads he would occasionally come after me with a flurry of smacks from the pads. I would hide behind my arms and just wait for him to get bored. I would have preferred to have a technique where I actually got right out of the way.

I'd noticed how a lot of the other fighters seemed to

be good at dodging blows. I wondered if this would be something I would have picked up in a beginner's class. Other people also had techniques for trapping kicks. I'd been shown how to trap a front kick once, but by the time I got a chance to practise it again I'd forgotten how it worked. I kept meaning to ask a trainer to refresh my memory, but these days they always seemed so busy it could be hard to get time with anyone for explanations.

So even though I approached my next sparring session with a more sensible attitude my defensive arsenal appeared embarrassingly low. Still I'd make the best use of what I had. There was no way I wanted to keep on going home and scaring my son. I knew that bruises and injuries were going to come again in the future, but I needed to limit them and not see them as a badge of honour. At the moment it appeared like I belonged to some vicious fight club where people fought bare knuckled.

I managed to get to the next session at Sitsongpeenong early; right before the sparring had even started. My wife had agreed to pick Timmy up from school in a taxi. I felt keen to find out if thinking defensively would make much difference. I wanted to be able to attack without paying for it with a lot of damage to my own face.

For my first opponent the trainer paired me up against a woman who looked to be in her twenties. I'd never fought a female before, and I felt uncomfortable with the idea. I'd seen this particular woman around the gym quite few times. I knew that she was highly skilled, but it just felt wrong to fight with her as if she was a man. She no doubt had more skill than me, but I still felt obliged to take it easy on her because of her sex.

She had a look of determination as she faced me; the same sort of look I'd seen on Marcus' face before he would knock me around the ring. Her gum shield gave her normally attractive face quite a sinister look. I tried to tap her gloves in a friendly manner, but she had already started throwing punches. They were hard and she came at me fast – like she wanted an instant knockout instead of some sparring. I tried my best to slow things down. I hoped that by holding back on the power of my punches it would encourage her to do the same. It didn't. As far as she was concerned she had got into the ring to spar and she didn't need any favours from me.

I tried to focus on my defensive techniques, but I kept on blocking too late. I increased the power of my blows slightly hoping that this would encourage her to back off, but it didn't. She dominated me and looked to be enjoying herself, but I continued to hold back. A couple of her punches really rocked me, and I had to struggle hard to keep on my feet. It came as a huge relief for the round to end.

We were meant to change partners, but once again I found myself with nobody new to fight. Everyone had already been paired up, and there was only me and this girl left standing without an opponent. I really didn't want to do another round with her. I'd made up my mind to work on my defensive technique but this had been taking the piss. Not only was she better than me, but I also felt unable to attack her with any type of conviction. This fight had put me in an uncomfortable dilemma. I felt that by holding back this could be interpreted as patronising, but by not holding back I'd feel like a bit of a monster. My lack of commitment to the sparring meant that she could knock me around – so much for my plan to avoid more injuries. Thankfully one of the trainers split up another group so that we would have new partners.

My next opponent looked to be an easy match-up for me after the girl, but he turned out to be a tough customer. He had a lot of muscle but didn't look too intimidating because of his childish face. He'd been at Sitsongpeenong a few weeks already and seemed to be a bit of a joker. I'd never really noticed him spar so I'd no idea what to expect from him; I hoped that his normally laid back attitude at the gym would make him a joy to spar with. I did know that he would be fighting at the end of the week and he'd noticeably increased the intensity of his training. He usually smiled a lot but in recent days had become a lot more serious about things.

The fight started off well. I concentrated on my block but I managed to get a few blows in on him as well. He looked really tense, and I guessed that the pre-fight nerves were starting to get to him. I managed to let off a flurry of punches, and for a couple of seconds I thought that I'd the upper hand in the fight. Then he came at me with punches of his own; heavy hooks that really shook me. I had no idea how to defend against these. I just hid underneath my arms, but this did not guard the side of my head. He kept on jabbing at my face and then following this up with more hooks.

I decided that my flimsy defence tactics weren't going to work for me against this guy. This felt too much like my earlier experiences with Marcus. I didn't want to be anyone's punch bag anymore so I abandoned defence and just concentrated on hitting him. My logic was that if he was being hit then he couldn't be hitting me. The harder I punched him though, the harder he came after me. The two of us stopped trying to defend and just began slugging each other. At one point we were going after each other so hard that the trainers pulled us apart. I had a ringing in my ear from his hooks, and I felt nauseous but not afraid. On more than a few occasions I felt as if his blows were about to knock me out. One of my punches managed to cut his lip, but it didn't do much to slow him down. I asked if he was OK, but he was in no mood for chit chat. The round seemed to go on forever.

I felt shook up from the round with smiley face. There were certainly moments when I'd enjoyed the action, but one of us could have been seriously damaged. We had been pounding each other's heads and that can't be good for anyone. I had a couple more rounds of sparring that day, but luckily for me they were nowhere as intense as the first two. I no longer enjoyed being hit, and I just wanted out of the ring. I once again wondered what madness had made me want to fight Muay Thai.

Chapter 34

THE FINAL BLOW TO MY plan to fight in 2011 came in late September. Maybe if I'd been more honest with myself I'd have seen it coming. I'd now reached a stage where I no longer wanted to fight, but was just continuing on the path out of a sense of obligation. I had increased the intensity of my training with the intention of being ready to fight at short notice, and I now made it to Sitsongpeenong four times a week. I no longer enjoyed it, and I couldn't see an end in sight. I deeply regretted not taking the fight that had been offered a few weeks previously. Even if I had received a bit of a beating it would be better than being trapped in an endless holding pattern.

I knew that my attitude of just wanting to get the fight out of the way wasn't making things easier. Instead of being a goal that would bring me joy at accomplishing it, it had become something to get beyond so that I could get back to my life. I'd spent so much of my time over the last six months thinking and worrying about fighting Muay Thai – even my dreams were always about fighting these days. I had enough and just wanted it to end.

It was a Thursday afternoon when I finally gave up on my goal to fight Muay Thai. It had been an uneventful training session. Once again there seemed to be a whole new crowd of foreigners at the camp. The session had been unremarkable until we got to clinching; mentally I was already in my car and driving home. I no longer saw Plam Muay as such a big deal. I would still occasionally get thrown around the ring, but I had developed a few techniques that would work for me in the clinch. I had definitely improved even if my skills were not going to impress too many people.

My clinching partner that day was quite a bit heavier than me but about the same height. He looked anxious and eager, but this is common for new people at the gym. I knew that within a couple of days he would gain more confidence and by then he would be telling me how my technique sucked. We started clinching but it felt like trying to tackle a stone statue – his body was so tense. Worst of all he had started using his strength rather than any type of technique. His weight against my neck felt painful. He landed a knee, and it was a lot harder than it should have been. In clinching we are only meant to tap each other because there is just too much risk of causing damage to the ribs. He should have known that.

My opponent stopped clinching and climbed out of the ring without a word. I hadn't even managed to land a knee on him so it seemed unlikely that he would have decided to call it a day. He rummaged through his sports bag at the side of the ring until he retrieved a gum shield. Most people don't bother with this protection while clinching but obviously this guy meant business. He had a renewed look of determination on his face when he returned.

We had only just restarted clinching when my opponent rammed the spike of his knee into my ribs. I doubled over in pain. One of the trainers noticed the strike and shouted out at my opponent to be careful. This warning came too late though. Once again my ribs were damaged. I felt upset and angry. I felt pissed off with this guy for going at me like a bull in a china shop, and I felt annoyed with the trainers for putting me clinching with someone so tense and so much heavier than me. Most of all I felt annoyed with my lack of assertiveness. I should have said something right away to my opponent when I first noticed that he was going too hard.

The trainer who had been monitoring the action came over and split us apart. We were both given new partners. I continued to clinch with somebody more my size. This turned out to be more of a battle of wits as we both tried to gain dominance. I found it hard to concentrate because I was worried about my ribs. The pain felt bearable now, but there hadn't been much discomfort initially after I'd damage my ribs the first time either. I tried to be positive, maybe this wouldn't be as bad as last time, but a black mood had taken over my thinking. I knew in my heart that this would mean another couple of months of Jep Sii Krong, and a huge setback in my preparations. I'd had enough and gave up on my plans to fight Muay Thai right then.

Chapter 35

I GAVE UP ON MY plans to fight but this didn't mean walking away from Muay Thai. Without the pressure to compete I started to have fun again. Instead of being focused on getting ready for a fight I directed my attention towards technique. This had been the thing that attracted me most about martial arts to begin with; focusing on movements to gain a sense of mastery over my body.

I could see that Muay Thai would be a great path for lifelong physical fitness. Private lessons weren't enough for me, but if I could attend the regular class a couple of times a week then this would be sustainable. I might even try to locate a class where they taught traditional Muay Thai.

Although I had given up on my preparations this did not mean that I'd closed the door on fighting Muay Thai completely. It just wasn't on my 'to do' list anymore. I could see now that attempting the fight within such a short time frame had been a mistake. One of the commentators on my blog made a great point when he said that I'd been putting the cart before the horse. The training should lead naturally to a fight and pushing things doesn't work. I had wanted a good ending for my book so I'd been trying to rush things along. My naive idea that it would be possible for me to progress faster than most people in Muay Thai didn't prove fruitful. If anything, my progress appeared to be slower than the average.

I returned to classes at Sitsongpeenong with no expectations of it building up to anything. I had no intention of doing any type of sparring until my ribs healed again. My focus now would be purely on technique. The summer had ended back in the West and only a handful of foreigners remained at the camp. The trainers now had a lot more time to offer one to one attention. I came to the realisation that I needed to be more proactive in my attempts to improve my technique.

Up until now the only time I'd asked questions would be while doing pads; my motive then would often be to slow things down rather than learn anything new. I now started to quiz the trainers about the exact details of each movement. Before this I'd worried that they might get annoyed with too many questions, but they went out of their way to share their knowledge with me. Even the Thai fighters were happy to explain techniques – all I needed to do was ask.

I became a bit obsessed with the details of each Muay Thai technique; the deeper I looked the more there was for me to learn. I became fascinated with how a tiny alteration to my body mechanics could make such a profound difference to the overall strike. By being more focused on the tiny details I could feel myself become more at one with the movements. One day while shadow boxing I became aware that my techniques were flowing into one another effortlessly.

I felt a sense of mastery over my body and for a few minutes I experienced Mushin – the empty mind that comes with being caught up in the flow. This is what I really wanted from a martial art and now I'd found it.

This book did not turn out as expected. I wanted to inspire people with a story of how a middle-aged ex-drunk could achieve something remarkable. I expected to leave the reader cheering me on to victory in the final chapter. This is the destination I set out to reach at the start of my expedition into Muay Thai, but it is not where the journey took me. Here we are at the end of the book though, and I'm still no closer to a fight than I was in the beginning.

My voyage into Muay Thai hasn't disappointed me. I know that it is still not over. My love for martial arts hasn't wavered throughout this journey, but I may have to accept that I'm no fighter. I can live with that. I can still find plenty within Muay Thai to keep me interested.